Still Standing

For the brave
women of Zambia.

Written by Wendy Machin
Compiled by Melissa Muldoon
Copyright © 2024 Wendy Machin

All rights reserved.
ISBN - 9798322725145

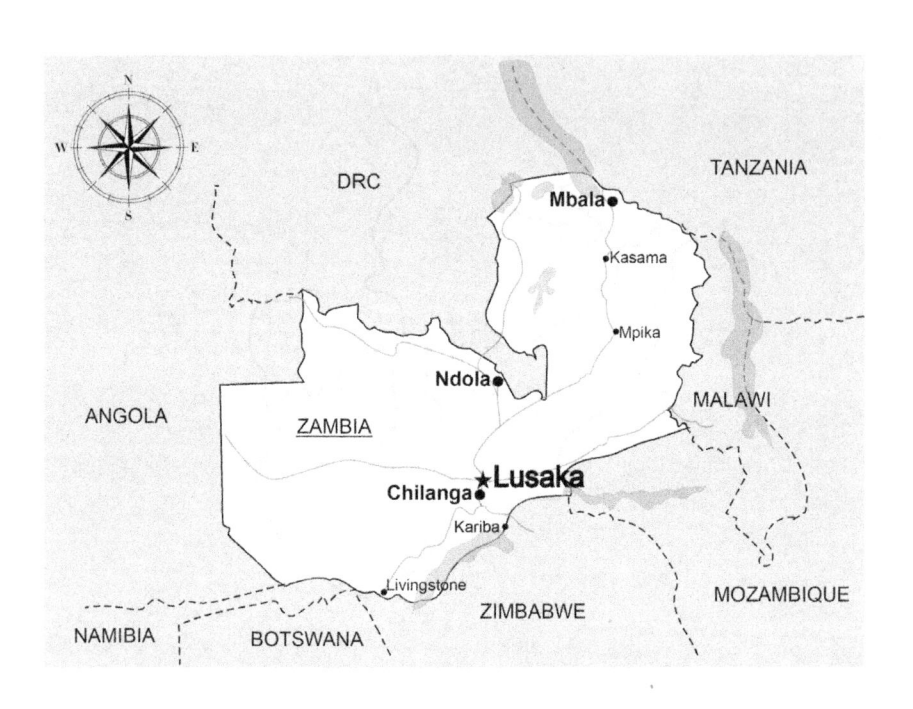

Still Standing

Prologue

"When an old person dies, a whole library burns" I came across this quotation from an African proverb recently, when talking to some friends about writing. Although I am hoping not to die any time soon, my mind flew to the boxes of diaries, reports and letters languishing in a cupboard at home. They describe more than twenty years of travels, visits and work in Zambia. They describe some of the amazing people we met, and some of the triumphs and disasters of those years. I hope you enjoy the story.

Our first contact was through a group of religious Sisters. While teaching social work in Liverpool, in 1996, Alan had got to know one of the Sisters, who was a headteacher at a local school for children with disabilities. When she moved to work in Zambia, Sr Elizabeth invited us to visit and we spent a few weeks staying with the small community of Sisters who were nurses and teachers in Lusaka. We were immediately drawn to the country and its people. It was a life changing experience for us and we have been going back there ever since.

A few months later, we packed up our house, said goodbye to our families and friends and went off to live in Zambia for a year. We were not Catholics or even religious, so everyone was surprised. We were surprised ourselves, yet somehow it seemed to work. Looking back, I can see that we had absolutely no idea what we were getting into. It did feel very strange at first, but we came to admire and respect these women, who were working in difficult conditions with the poorest people in the townships. Our work with the Sisters of this religious order involved visiting all the projects they had established over many years, in different areas of Zambia and talking to community members, staff and volunteers. We were working as volunteers ourselves, but they supported us for our daily needs and provided us with a small van to travel around the country. At the end of the year we were asked to produce a report, with observations and recommendations for the way forward. Our remit was not religious in any way, but developmental, looking at their work in education, health and community development. It was both a privilege and a responsibility to take this on, but we did our very best. Along the way we got to know the country, as we visited various regions and began to understand something of the history and different cultures of Zambia.

We had many interesting and inspiring experiences that first year and developed a love for the country and its people. I have described here something of what followed, when we got together with a group of friends and set out to help some of the poorest Zambian families and children from our home in the UK. We started with high hopes and a few too many ideals, probably naïve and unrealistic. Unsurprisingly, we had setbacks and disappointments, but, along the way, we made some good friends, offered help to people wherever we could and learned a lot.

I have included some anecdotes from my diaries, written during our regular visits to Zambia and some observations from family, colleagues and friends who were there with us at various times. Looking back, there are plenty of things we might have done differently if we had known more about the country and the different traditions, culture and beliefs of the people we worked with. Our starting point was to try to treat everyone with kindness, friendliness and respect, regardless of who they were. You have to start somewhere.

One of the most influential people we worked with was Hellen Mpundu. I met her when we first went to the Copperbelt area, and she and I became friends. Much of what I have written is about her work and her ideals and what we tried to achieve together. Hellen continues to live and work with one of the poorest communities in Zambia. She has experienced many problems and opposition, but she has not been cowed by adversity but carried on regardless and remained strong. Even when faced with the near collapse of everything we worked for together, she has come up with solutions and made the most of whatever opportunities came along. Hellen and I spent some time together in Lusaka recently, looking back at things that happened to us. We talked together as two retired women, as we promised each other long ago that we would. But Hellen has not retired! She is back at the community school we started together in 2001, still full of enthusiasm and energy and humour. Still strong and determined. Still standing.

There have been many other people involved in the Families for Children Zambia project and we have been so lucky to have a strong and supportive UK team. Some members of the team came to Zambia to work with us, while others were fundraising and organizing things back home.

All the names of people mentioned have been changed, unless they have given their permission to be identified.

Zambia was a different country when we arrived in the mid-nineties, with less traffic, fewer roads, fewer shopping malls and filling stations and buildings. But the country was broken economically, it was in the deadly grip of an AIDS pandemic, which had decimated the child rearing age group and there were more than a million orphan children.

It was only just over 30 years since Zambia had become independent and it was still finding its way as a nation, freeing itself from the colonial past. It was one of the poorest countries in the world, with few decent roads, railways or other transport links and many commodities were scarce. There was very high unemployment and the main urban areas of the Copperbelt and

Lusaka were crowded with people who had come looking for work. Some were employed in the mines or in domestic service, but otherwise they lived mostly in townships (compounds), where they scraped a living by any means available. People in rural villages were largely dependent on subsistence farming. Despite all these hardships and poverty, we found most of the Zambians we met were warm, friendly and sociable. We were constantly amazed by their resourcefulness and how they managed to survive, with so little.

Hellen with Wendy

Chapter 1

I wake up, confused, after a long, restless night. The small bedroom is infused with golden light, through the thin curtains. There are burglar bars on the windows, a narrow bed, wooden chair and bare floor. Where am I? As my mind struggles free from the clouds of dreams, I remember. I am in Zambia, in a religious community. How can that be?

Soon I will be going home, to take up my life again, do what can be done to help, from a distance. I enjoy being with the women and children here and find them inspiring. I will be sad to leave, but this is my decision - or is it?

As I lie thinking, I count off all the reasons why it would be a bad idea to move to Zambia:

A comfortable home that I love back in England

A family and many good friends there

A rewarding job that I love

I'm wary of religious institutions

Elderly relatives will be upset

Two dogs will have to be rehomed.

There are plenty more reasons

Yet somehow it seems that the decision is already made. So many apparently random things have led me to this place. I'm doing it anyway. I'm going to come back.

The sun is already high and bright as we circle the airport, peering down through eyes grainy with sleep at Africa, golden and brown like an old map beneath us. Huddles of small houses come into view, beyond the perimeter fence, then a low line of airport buildings. I am nervous and excited as I climb down the steps of the aircraft, with Alan, into the warm wind, and walk across the tarmac.

We join a straggling line of people in the customs hall, feeling conspicuous among a crowd of black faces. Notices proclaim 'residents, visitors and VIPs' and we hesitate, unsure which line to join, to get our visas. But help is at hand: a stout, African nun sails towards us and asks us, in good English, if we need help. She guides us to one of the lines and we wait anxiously for a Zambian official to take our details and issue a visa. I am anticipating problems, as we approach the customs exit. A young white couple with a small baby, ahead of us, empty everything from their cases and the floor is strewn with their stuff, as the baby screams, the mother cries, and the young father loses his temper. Out in the car park, we are besieged by taxi drivers, who seize our luggage and make off with it. We try to keep up, as our luggage trolley speeds ahead of us. After some heated negotiation between competing drivers, we find ourselves, at last, in a battered taxi with a soldered crack across the windscreen.

We pass through the outskirts of Lusaka, on the way from the airport. There is burnt grass, occasional trees, dusty roads lined with wide verges and walls bearing slogans and adverts painted by hand. 'Save Lusaka for Jesus', 'Mosi beer of Zambia' 'Drink Fanta'.

Many people are walking, walking beside the road, or in the road, some on bicycles, laden with stuff – bags of maize, bundles of charcoal, pots and pans. There are few cars, and most that we see are Toyota trucks, or beat up taxis, held together with string and solder. Some lorries seem to be proceeding crabwise, at an angle to the road. The well surfaced airport road ends abruptly as we reach the suburbs of the city. The road soon deteriorates into an obstacle course of potholes, bordered on both sides by deep rain ditches.

We pass through a township, a dirty, noisy, crowded place, but full of activity. Tyre mending, welding, carpentry and brick making, is happening everywhere. Piles of bricks, stones, furniture, coffins, and wire toys are on sale on the side of the road. There are small houses of mud brick with tin roofs, children running around, people sitting on their steps, music blasting out from the taverns. We pass through at a slow pace, being accosted frequently by hopeful salespeople, offering multiple choices, should we wish to eat, drink, repair a car, build a house or buy a table. On the dry wind is the smell of cooking fires, charcoal and petrol. I have my window open, to take in all the sights and sounds and smells, but our driver is not in favour of this.

"No madam, please close your window, make sure your bag is under the seat. There are thieves here."

We continue, through a more affluent district, which has large houses standing back from the road, with well-tended green lawns in front, high walls and locked gates. There are flamboyant trees with brilliant scarlet blooms and bougainvillea bursting over walls, topped with barbed wire or broken glass. Guards patrol outside and dogs bark within.

On another suburban road of more modest dwellings, we come to the house where we are to stay in Zambia. Initially we are sharing accommodation, with a small community of Catholic Sisters. As we drive into the gates, we see a large bungalow, set back from the road in a pleasant garden, with, trees, flowers and vegetables growing. There is a shady veranda across the front, with chairs and a table. There are other buildings at the side of the drive, which we later find are offices and guest accommodation. We are happy to see that it looks as it does, well-tended and neat, but friendly as well, just an ordinary family home, really. In fact this is exactly what it had been until a year or two previously when it was bought by the religious order we were to work with. I don't know quite what I had been expecting, but maybe a large institutional building with a chapel and religious iconography? Anyway, I am happy to be here. Two of the Sisters soon come out to greet us, to help us unload all our stuff and to make us a very welcome cup of tea.

We have a bedroom with a desk, a chair, a cupboard, two beds and access to a bathroom. No kitchen, but we are to take our meals with the Sisters in the main house. Because we are close to the equator, when darkness falls, it is as if someone has turned a rapid dimmer switch and suddenly the night is full of sounds: frogs, cicadas, distant music, and occasional cars passing. As we cross the garden, we look up at the night sky, to see if the southern cross is visible. It isn't because the lights are too bright, but it is thrilling to know that it is there somewhere.

Chapter 2

Getting to work

My first job was in the township, close to where we were staying on the outskirts of Lusaka. The Sisters had established themselves in that area only a year or two before we arrived, and I got involved with their work with disabled children. I was wondering what I could offer to these people, about whom I knew so little, but I began visiting the families with a local woman, a teacher: I was ready to learn from her and to get to know the parents of children with disabilities. These children were often kept hidden at home and shunned by their community. Back home, in Chester, England, I had helped to set up a centre for families who had children with severe learning disabilities. Without exception, our Chester families all wanted their children to have an education and to be able to make friends and be accepted, just like any other children, so it was not a big surprise to find that most of these Zambian mothers (it was usually women we talked to) wanted similar things. How could we help? The first step was to establish a class for disabled children at the local school. This was just getting going when I arrived and it was so heartening to find the children waiting for us with big smiles, eager to learn, as soon as we had cleaned out the dusty room and put out the toys and materials we brought with us.

My first visits to the compound were quite a culture shock. Most of the houses were small, built of mud bricks and crowded together, with narrow pathways between. The pit latrines were often shared between a few families. As I went around on my bicycle, visiting families and going into their homes, I was dismayed to see the levels of poverty and lack of basic facilities that existed.

From my diary

Rainstorm. Rivers of mud from the overflowing rain ditches. I hitched up my skirt and wheeled my bike through. I reached Rita's little house, just one room, and sat inside on a small stool, as rain drummed on the roof so loud that we could hardly hear each other. This was supposed to be a language lesson for me to learn Nyanja, but no chance! There was a little boy with a broken arm carrying a charcoal brazier, just by my feet and the baby touching it – poking in bits of paper – so dangerous! Rita's son died of burns from boiling water quite recently. Rita's voice was expressionless as she told me about it. Her older daughter was at school. She is bright but she has no light at night to read or do anything by. Must take her some candles tomorrow. Candles are probably dangerous too. Rita told us previously that her husband, Ken, who is a good man, gentle and kind, had never been officially registered. He is unable to get medical treatment or regular work without registration.

The following day I went to collect Rita and Ken, in the van. They had changed into their best clothes. We drove into Lusaka to the BOMA (DSS Social Welfare and Registrar's office) It is an awful place in downtown Lusaka - dark, crowded. Nobody seemed to know what was going on or what Ken must do to get himself registered. He didn't know his exact age or when and where he was born. We sat with a crowd of people, who were waiting with remarkable patience for a bored looking official to call someone to a window to speak to him. Meanwhile, the official shuffled papers, wandered off and chatted with his colleagues and returned at a leisurely pace. After a long wait, we left Ken there for a few more hours and returned to pick him up later but he still didn't manage to get it sorted. On the way back we visited Rita's parents' home, to pick up the children. They live in another compound, which is larger and even more noisy and crowded.

We drove back in the fierce heat of the afternoon to see the Nativity play at the special needs unit for disabled children. The room was crowded with parents and carers, sitting on dusty benches, waiting to see the show. The light filtered through the dirty windows, illuminating the dust floating in the air. Joseph was played by a little boy with a wooden leg and the Innkeeper, little Freddy, who was deaf, came to sit on our knees. Mary dropped the baby Jesus, to gasps from the audience and she scrambled to pick him up again, swinging him by one arm. There were babies crawling around the dusty floor, children laughing and dancing, two ragged, giggling girls, full of mischief, with shining eyes. Despite all the difficulties, it was a joyful occasion.

Bauleni Township in the 1990s

Other work in Zambia

The Sisters had a wide network of contacts and friends throughout Zambia and people soon got to know when we were there and to ask for our help. Training in social work, and management seemed to be in demand, and people were keen to gain knowledge. We did our best to make the materials we had to offer, more relevant, becoming better at this, the more we learned from Zambian people about their culture and beliefs.

The sun set at 18.00 hours every evening and there was no TV, radio or internet so the nights did seem very long and there was plenty of time to work, although the power went off quite frequently. In Lusaka, at the time, there was an arrangement known as 'power sharing', which involved different areas having their electricity cut off, at random times. Anyway, we had plenty to occupy us, and we worked through the long, dark evenings in our room, preparing materials, after the sun had set. We enjoyed the work, though some of our ideas, especially on management, could be a source of great amusement and probably did not fit at all with Zambia cultural practices at the time.

The sessions we led on staff recruitment and selection were classic. We tried to explain, for our students, how to prepare job descriptions, and how to conduct interviews with applicants which were fair and unbiased. We decided that role playing the parts of interviewer and interviewee would a good way to demonstrate some of the issues involved and came up with various scenarios: for example, the interviewee who was too nervous to talk, the one who talked too much but didn't answer any questions, the interviewer who was too intimidating or too chatty. Our course participants took a great delight in this and found it all very funny. They were always keen to volunteer for acting the various parts and did so with great gusto, hamming it up, to raise a laugh. But although they enjoyed the sessions, it was obvious that they thought our ideas were crazy and would never work.

"What, appoint someone you don't even know?"

"How can you trust someone who is not from your family or your religion?"

"Everyone knows you should never trust a stranger."

We had some laughs in these sessions and discovered that people shared our sense of humour, taking a great delight in mimicking us and parodying our mannerisms, as we tried to keep a straight face, getting a message across!

We had many discussions on the rights of children and protecting children from abuse and neglect. Most people agreed with this in theory, but the reality was often very different. At the time Zambia had just signed up to an international treaty on the rights of the child and there was interest (in some quarters) on how to put this into practice. We were asked to lead courses on child protection for childcare organisations in Lusaka, which seemed to go down well, but we were doubtful how much our course students really understood. Many did not speak much English and we were dependent on the services of a local interpreter, who took a very long time to explain things, with much arm waving and dramatic gestures. We were not at all sure what he was communicating to the students, but they seemed to enjoy the courses and gave us great feedback.

There was a large UNICEF office in Lusaka and they requested some training for The Zambian Police Victim Support Unit. They asked us for specific training on interviewing and protecting vulnerable children. Officers from all regions were to attend a week long course in Lusaka and we were very apprehensive about this. We asked a friend who was visiting us from England, a few weeks beforehand, to bring out a pack of training materials on Child Abuse and Neglect which had been very recently produced by the Open University, so it was bang up to date. We studied it night and day for weeks, before conducting the training but felt we were by no means experts. However, the course was an excellent one and contained video tapes and audio tapes as well as a wide variety of materials we could choose from.

On the day we arrived at the police training college, we were nervous. We were welcomed formally by a committee of high-ranking officers in uniform and treated to a performance by the police band. We felt like VIPs and found it very embarrassing, especially when we saw ourselves on the TV news later that evening.

We were only too aware that we had a limited knowledge of the conditions, the custom law and the traditions and superstitions that many of these officers were dealing with in their different communities. We hoped our skills and experience, gained in the UK, would be helpful and they had asked us to share it with them, so this is what we did. We certainly learned a lot and I think our police officers did too.

Although we couldn't hope to gain a thorough knowledge of the Zambian legal system during a few weeks, the research we had done made it clear that there were considerable unresolved difficulties. In effect, there was a dual legal reality. The statute law, mainly inherited from the British system, written down and enshrined in the constitution of Zambia, was largely unknown to many people at the time. Only a small number of people, especially in rural areas, had been given the opportunity for secondary education. Customary law, which was handed down by oral tradition, but widely known and applied locally, was what most people lived by. We were advised that 'Local court' judges in rural areas were elected by the tribe and were supposed to make rulings in accordance with the traditions of the tribe.

Some of the police officers described situations of child abduction, abuse and the seizing of property when a woman was widowed, which were unjust, but which were well known in Zambia. They also had to deal with issues of witchcraft, which they tried to explain to us in a very open and informative way. There were other examples, relevant to issues of child protection and abuse, child labour and early marriages and domestic abuse. Beating of both women and children seemed to be widely accepted, and police officers recounted incidents where they had to go in a group, armed to the teeth, to deal with offences against women or children because people in the community would not support them.

We found that many of these police officers had a good sense of humour and great patience in explaining things to us and we enjoyed the week we spent with them. One of the women I remember especially well. She was a large, strong, woman, who always had plenty to say. She assured us that she had no problem in dealing with male offenders who had been mistreating their wives or children.

"So what do you do?" we asked her. "Oh, I just beat them," she replied!

The insights we gained from this course helped us to understand the challenges faced by brave people like Hellen Mpundu, who was trying to help women to protect themselves and their children: she was seen as a threat by those in power.

In the Northern Province

During our years coming and going in Zambia, we continued to do some work for the Sisters, from time to time. On a few occasions Alan and I had the opportunity to work in the Northern Province, way up near the border with Tanzania, on the shores of Lake Tanganyika. Here we stayed in a small house in a compound, close to a large religious community, where several Sisters were living, together with trainees and volunteers.

The Sisters and volunteers were working on various projects, mostly with sick people and orphan children but also in rural villages, encouraging the development of sustainable agricultural practices. Our courses were about children, their rights, their needs and how best to help children who had been abused or neglected or bereaved. Some of the subjects discussed were culturally very difficult and sensitive for people to address and it could be emotionally exhausting at times. We had our own little house there and people would often come and see us whenever they could manage to get away for a private chat. Looking back on my diaries, I can see that we had company most evenings. I don't know how we managed to feed people, as there was precious little choice of food available in the local market and we seemed to subsist for quite long periods on tomatoes, sweet potatoes and rice.

Sometimes we had fish, from the market in Mpulungu, on the shores of Lake Tanganyika, where fish was sold daily from the small boats on the lake. It was a few miles drive down a steep hill to the lake and it was always oppressively hot there in the valley. Mpulungu was a place where African and Arab influences mingled, as the enormous lake formed part of a waterway, connecting the centre of Africa with the East coast. It also bordered the Democratic Republic of Congo (which at that time was known as Zaire). This connected it with the culture, music and fashion, foods and textiles of different countries and regions and many goods were traded there. We enjoyed watching the people, the water and the lakeside life. The lake shore was always full of activity, noise and colour, as small boats were beached on the sand and fish was unloaded directly onto sheets of plastic or tarpaulins. Small boys swam around and played in the water, fishermen and traders shouted their wares. Women hawked bright cloths and other goods. To me it looked chaotic and had an edge of danger and there was no shade or shelter from the blinding sun. After a visit there we were always pleased to return to the much cooler and more pleasant temperatures in Mbala.

Lake shore Mpulungu near Mbala

From my Diary

May 25th. My birthday. We had a restless night in a house by the lake. Very hot and plenty of mosquitoes. Got up and had a cold shower. We drove back up the hill to Mbala, to collect a picnic and borrowed the 4-wheel drive community car. Set off for Kalambo falls. We drove slowly through the main street, as shopkeepers were opening up for the day. Passed a young boy with a piglet in his arms and another with a massive load of charcoal on the crossbar of his bike. The road passed through tall grasses and sparse woodlands. We kept stopping to give lifts to people along the way. We came eventually to a wooded hillside full of rocks, which opened into an enormous rift valley, with precipitous sides of soaring rock. Marabou storks were wheeling overhead, floating in the updraft. This was the edge of the great African rift valley, which cleft the land from Ethiopia to Mozambique.

An old man in a ragged shirt and trousers came out to greet us beside a cardboard sign saying 'Car Park'. It was described in the guide book as one of the wonders of Zambia, but we were the only people there. We parked up and edged our way to the edge of the cliff, where, by clinging to a tree and hanging over a rock, we were able to see the falls, a single stream of water, descending into the spray and the unfathomable depths. We scrambled up to where the Kalambo river flows gently to the edge of the cliff, then plunges 221 metres to the rocks below. It is twice as high as Victoria falls but just a single fall, the second highest in Africa. We watched the water for a long time, then climbed back up through the woodland for our picnic. It is said that there is evidence of the first fire used by humans in Africa, around this place, when our ancestors occupied the area 100,000 years ago or more and began using stone tools and weapons. Driving back past scattered houses, built of mud, with roughly thatched roofs, where people were digging the soil with hoes and sitting on bamboo mats, we pondered why this part of Africa has developed in the way it has.

Wendy, looking over the Kalambo Falls

During another visit we were asked by the Sisters to go north to Kasama. It was October, the hottest time of the year and we stopped on the way to break the journey, in Chilonga, at a large house, near Mpika. It had once been home to dozens of Sisters, who founded and worked in the hospital nearby. The hospital had long since been handed over to the government, so there were now only a few people remaining in the enormous house, which had many empty rooms. It was a peaceful place, and we were always made welcome there, at the end of a long drive north from Lusaka.

When we travelled on to Kasama, we spent some days at a residential home for children with disabilities. It was a government run institution and we were not impressed with it. The living conditions for the children were crowded, dirty and insanitary and the headteacher was an ineffectual man who seemed to attribute most of his problems to witchcraft! The children were wonderful, they supported each other, and the stronger ones looked after the weakest. Alan and I taught some courses on childcare, but we were not very hopeful that any of our suggestions would be implemented. It was exhausting work.

While there, I was unlucky enough to get malaria and it completely wiped me out. I have never felt so weak, exhausted and bad tempered, as my diaries reveal. I sweated and shivered alternately through the interminable nights in a small house which was unbearably hot and felt like a prison. It gave me the creeps to imagine those malaria parasites wriggling in my blood ! We were staying with a small community of Sisters, who looked after me very well and I am ashamed to have been so ungracious and irritable. I was left feeling strangely spaced out and unable to concentrate on anything, so it was just as well that we were due to return home the following week, after spending six weeks in the country. As soon as I was well enough we set off to return to Lusaka, a very long journey in a small van, down endless roads, full of potholes and almost empty of vehicles. At last we reached Chilonga, where again we stayed overnight.

Diary entry
We left in the early morning, after a sleepless night. It was cool at first, with the sun behind us. Beautiful trees and vistas across towards Luangwa, with kites and eagles soaring and sweeping over the road. Bikes with assorted loads, people, charcoal, pigs, sacks of maize, mattresses, grasses, three to a bike sometimes. Children running to the roadside with struggling chickens, bowls of wild fruits, men with bush meat and wild honeycomb. Only the brave collect honey from African bees. At Chilonga we walked up the hillside behind the house just before sunset. Standing up on the hill, beside a wooden cross, we looked out over the endless miles of bush, stretching out to the horizon. What was out there? Most of the villages are along the line of road and rail so there must be untouched virgin land with nothing and nobody for hundreds of miles.

Alan with our little van

Chapter 3

Meeting Hellen Mpundu

It was during our first year in Zambia that we first went to the Copperbelt, where we met Hellen, who was working with a community education project, to combat AIDS. At this time, many of the former cultural safeguards for bringing up children had been weakened, because of the effects of the AIDS pandemic. Very many people of child rearing age had died, and died rapidly, with no effective treatments available. The result was an enormous number of single or double orphans. Many were living with older siblings or elderly grandparents, who had no means of support. Thousands were living on the streets.

There were some damaging beliefs circulating about AIDS, which included the shameful idea that sex with a young child or a child with disabilities could cure or protect against disease. Misinformation, rumour and false beliefs multiplied and spread like wildfire, even in the press and government circles. We were amazed to see, in the daily newspapers, advertisements placed by 'Doctors' who claimed to cure or prevent AIDS by various fantastic means. They would make other promises too, such as the power to bring back errant husbands or provide aphrodisiacs for disappointed lovers or enable success at work!

The Sisters with whom we worked in the Copperbelt had established a project to educate people on health issues and safe sex. The message was taken to different sections of the community by Peer Educators, who worked directly with groups. For example, they worked with young people, the police, truck drivers, community schools and women's groups, sex workers and churches. While abstinence was the ideal, the project leaders were realistic enough to understand that saving lives was the greater priority and condoms were freely given out. Unfortunately, they were not always successfully used.

Hellen and I have been friends and colleagues ever since we met. In her I saw a woman who was not afraid to challenge authority, and to follow her own path. She has told me that she saw something similar in me. Hellen was a hard worker, whose priority was always to work, hands on, in the community, rather than talking and going to meetings. But, when she did speak, her passion and conviction made her a powerful force. We shared a commitment to children, doing our best to protect them and to give them a better chance in life, through education and the support of caring adults. This had been the focus of my work up to now and this was Hellen's too. It has always been a close bond between us.

Hellen's work was with community schools and groups of women in the Townships. She impressed me immediately with her independence and free spirit. She didn't always keep to the rules but had a love for the countryside and local culture, which took her into the heart of the poorest areas. She liked to wear traditional dress, which was unusual for educated young women, who mostly seemed to prefer Western style clothes, often bought at the markets, which did a roaring trade in Salaula or second-hand clothes, imported from overseas. She spoke English well enough but would use her native language, Bemba, whenever possible and she was not afraid to speak plainly and to express her opinions forcefully at times. Hellen was interested in traditional medicines and plants and cooking and she took me to places I would not otherwise have known.

From my diary
A beautiful fresh morning and I woke early. I drove to Kitwe to meet with Hellen at the education office. She took me out to a village near Luanshya, to meet a group there who are growing vegetables and groundnuts. We walked along a bush road, with

high grasses on either side, and then into the fields to look at the groundnuts and maize. We met a group in the village and walked down with them to the dam – shimmering water and water lilies – wind in the trees and tall grasses blowing above our heads. We sat under the shade of a tree and talked together.

Hellen talked about HIV/AIDS and hung posters on the trees. The group seemed to be waiting for a lesson from 'Auntie Hellen'. Some of them had babies on their backs, as they often did: it was rare to see a young woman without a child, either on her back or toddling beside her. After that Hellen lit a fire and showed the young women how to cook soya beans. There were some older people in the group and 3 or 4 men; everyone was very friendly and relaxed with us. A beautiful peaceful place and we were all reluctant to leave. On the way home I drove through a torrential downpour but found it dry back in Chingola

This is what Hellen told me about her life.

She was born in Kitwe, in the Copperbelt, in 1964, the year Zambia achieved independence from the British Colonial Government. The first President of the new country of Zambia was Kenneth Kaunda and hopes were high for a new era of freedom and equality and prosperity. Kaunda made great efforts to encourage a sense of unity and nationhood, despite the disparate nature of the country, which held numerous tribes with different customs and languages. There was a great potential for ethnic conflict, but the mantra for the new country was 'One Zambia one Nation' and most Zambian citizens were able to live with that.

The departing British Government had left a very flawed legacy. There were few Zambian personnel qualified to manage the essential services and businesses left behind. Many Zambians had received only a minimal education at primary level and were treated like second class citizens by most of the white people who occupied key posts in the government and civil service. Much of the industrial development in the country at the time was in the Copperbelt, and in these areas the inequality was very clear to see.

Hellen's father worked in the mines and his large family was housed in a very basic small house, while the white mine workers and supervisors had well-built bungalows, with large gardens. Black people were confined to the mean streets of their own townships and forbidden to go into the areas occupied by whites, which had shops, sports facilities, hospitals, tree lined roads and parks. Their wages and working conditions were poles apart. This felt like a kind of apartheid, and was, understandably, a cause of great anger and resentment among the black community. Hellen's father was a natural leader in his community. He was a man with a strong sense of justice and he spoke out against the unfairness of the system..

In her own words:
My father used to talk too much when he came home. He made me see how things were. Black people were so scared of the whites and they didn't speak up. They just kept to their own areas. The women were expected to stay home and look after their children, to respect their husbands and keep quiet. They were just there listening. They didn't say anything. Why didn't the women talk? But my father's talk made trouble for him and soon he was threatened. It was not safe for him to stay and he had to run away. He returned to the village.

This was a difficult time for Hellen, who had been doing well at her school in the Copperbelt. She had to go to the village in Luapula Province, together with her mother and her younger brothers and sisters. The older ones remained in Kitwe. There were 10 children in the family and Hellen was number six. She describes her mother as a very beautiful woman and a very strong woman, who encouraged her children to speak up for themselves. In the village Hellen's father had high status and owned land: he had a more traditional role within the community. Women and girls were expected to do much of the work within the family and girls did not often go to school. For Hellen this was very disappointing and very hard. She missed a year of school and was doing manual labour, fetching water and fuel, tilling the land, cooking and cleaning, looking after younger children. She was sent eventually to a boarding school, where she was very unhappy. Her mother always tried to encourage her but she did not do well and failed her exams.

Eventually one of her older brothers came to fetch her back to the Copperbelt so that she could look after his children and his house. Hellen married while still very young, to a man she met at her uncle's house; she saw this as an escape from a very difficult situation. Sadly, it did not work out that way …. Her husband brought many problems. She didn't want to me to write any more about what these were. But she had five children whom she loved dearly. She did the best she could within the marriage for some years, until her situation became unbearable, but she always remained and still remains close to her children.

Hellen was determined to take what opportunities she could to improve her life and to continue her education. She began by helping as a volunteer in a home-based care project, visiting and looking after very sick people. This brought her into contact with other women and she learned a lot from meeting many different people, while working in the community. She enrolled on courses at the local college whenever she could and became a passionate advocate for the rights of women and children.

By the mid 1990s Hellen was working as a peer educator and her main interest was in community schools. She understood the importance of education, especially to improve the position of women and girls and did whatever she could to promote and encourage this. The methods she used were typical of Hellen. She talked first with the women in the community, moving and working amongst them and gaining the trust and respect of even the most downtrodden and abused. She encouraged them to find their voice and to speak up for themselves. Where there were women there were also children and the overwhelming need for schooling became obvious. Government schools required school fees to be paid and a uniform to be worn, but most families could not afford this. The result was that many of the brightest and most promising children were denied an education.

At this time, cultural practices reinforced the idea that woman were subservient to men and I came across many examples of this.

From my diary
Alan and I were leading a course at the Copperbelt University on social work and management. The participants were a mixed group of people, mainly social workers and health workers, who all spoke good English, but the men always dominated the class discussions. At lunchtime, I joined a group of women, who were sitting outside, in the shade of a tree. They were talking animatedly. One of them was about to get married and they were speaking about the so called 'initiation' practices she will have to go through. These are designed to prepare young women for married life and include routine beating and humiliations of various kinds 'to strengthen and prepare them for what is to come'. Women are instructed to kneel before their father-in-law, when they bring his food or drink and to show deference to his demands. They also have instruction on how to please their husbands and keep them sexually satisfied, so that they will not take other women. There was quite a lot of detailed information, most of which sounded horrific to me. I asked Alan if young men had similar instructions or initiations before marriage, but nobody offered to share this information with him!

Chapter 4

Ruth and her orphan children

Looking back on the things that happened during our first year in Zambia, I can see that meeting with Ruth was a key event for us and led directly to the setting up of our charity 'Families for Children Zambia'. Ruth was introduced to us by one of the Sisters, who worked in the townships of the Copperbelt. Ruth had been a nurse in one of the mine hospitals, which was set up in colonial times, to care for workers in the copper mines, and their families. She was a trained nurse and a good one but, when I first met her, she was looking after orphan children in a small residential home in Ndola. I vividly remember the day Ruth invited me into that house and took me into the room where the children were in cots. The room was clean and tidy but there were many cots lining the walls and children were standing up in them, their eyes wide and guarded, as they watched us. Some of them were just babies, who had been abandoned soon after birth and the future for them did not look promising. The children were well fed and clean, but their eyes were haunted. There were not enough people to give them individual attention and they had learned not to cry. Their lives had taught them that nobody would come to help them. It was heart-breaking.

Ruth explained that there was little chance of neighbours or family members taking on these children, when so many people had died or were very sick. She was looking for alternative ways of caring for them and was hoping to find foster families, who could be trained and given some help to do this. There was no system for supporting foster carers or adopters in Zambia at that time and Ruth herself had been the first person to adopt a child, a few years before, a boy she had found abandoned, when he was a newborn baby.

I had worked in a fostering and adoption team in the UK and Ruth asked me if I could help her to see if something like it could be developed in her area. Ruth reminded me of Hellen Mpundu, in that she was interested in preserving what was good from traditional culture as well as learning from the new. She had firm ideas on the rights and needs of children, and I soon discovered that the two women knew each other and were friends.

After that first meeting, we arranged for Ruth to come and stay with us for a few weeks, in England, to find out more about fostering and adoption. While she was with us, she worked diligently, learning as much as she could. We had some interesting times together and we took her around to see parts of England and Wales. She was fascinated by the sea and awed by the majesty of the Welsh mountains; their slopes appearing, hung with gauzy curtains of drifting cloud, as we drove through a high mountain pass.

Ruth also spent some time teaching us some words in Bemba, her local language and giving us tips on cultural beliefs and practices, which varied enormously, according to tribal traditions. We talked to her about the still widespread belief in witchcraft, which seemed to exist in Zambia alongside the Christian faith. At the time Ruth was with us, we also had an African friend from Cameroon staying with us and our evenings were lively with their discussions of different customs and beliefs. We asked a lot of questions and were astonished by some of the things they told us: Ruth was very generous in sharing her knowledge. We seldom had the opportunity to talk to anyone as frankly and honestly as this. She opened our eyes to many things, and we kept in touch with her when she left, although this was not straightforward in those days. The internet was not widely available, and few people had functioning phones or land lines. Letters were the main means of communication, and the mail often took weeks to arrive. At the end of her time with us, Ruth took a case full of training materials and books that she had been given and she made good use of them when she got back to her own country.

We visited Zambia again early in 2000 to see Ruth. By this time she had several orphans and vulnerable children living with her and we spent some time with her and with Hellen Mpundu, who was still working with the Health Education project in the Copperbelt. The two women had similar ideals and ways of working. It was good to see that Ruth had benefitted from her visit to England and had set up another facility for young children, a kind of pre-school, in the town of Ndola. She was always keen to focus on the needs of young children and this was also a priority for Hellen and for me too. All of us understood the vital needs of young children for a good, stable relationship with a carer, for protection from harm and for opportunities to learn and develop.

In traditional Zambian societies, babies and very young children were seldom more than an arm's length from their mothers. They were either tied onto their mother's or carer's back or toddling beside, but the bond was strong and I believe this gave them a secure basis to build on, when difficult times occurred later in life. They also had other female relatives who would look after them at times and many 'Aunties' within their village or community. But this structure was decimated by the AIDS pandemic, which took the lives of so many people of child rearing age, leaving only elderly grandmothers or older siblings to care for little ones. Hellen always said "It takes a whole village to raise a child". But at this time, neighbours who might have taken in orphaned children were already struggling to survive and to care for their own families and had nothing left to give. The idea of paying foster carers was a good one in principle, but there were many obstacles in the way of putting this into practice and, sadly, Ruth did not live long enough to achieve her aims.

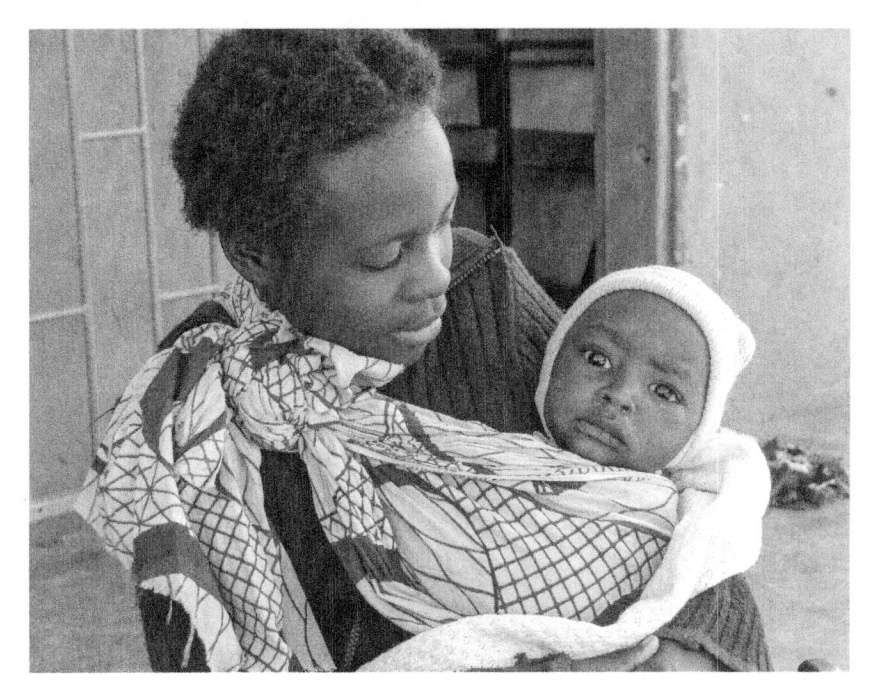

During this visit, Alan and I stayed in a local guest house, which was basic, but very comfortable in comparison with the conditions in the compounds. It felt safe enough there in the daytime, when it was mainly women and children who were around: they would be getting on with their work, fetching water and firewood, minding the little children, cooking at small roadside stalls, sometimes calling out to us to buy things. But by night the area belonged to the men. Most of the houses and the narrow roads were in darkness. Only the taverns and bars were well lit, with loud music, raised voices and drunken men stumbling around. Fights frequently broke out, or so we were told.

I had a very scary experience one night driving in a borrowed van.

From my diary
Ruth visited me at the guest house where we are staying, and darkness fell before we realised how late it was. The house where she lives is on the outer fringes of the township and has a small

garden, where she grows some vegetables.

"Why don't I take you home in the van?" I suggested.

"No, Wendy, you know it's not safe at night."

"Well, I'll be driving, I'll lock the doors and windows, what can happen to me? I won't stop for anyone, and I will look very fierce!"

"Okay then but please be careful, I'm serious. It's not a good place at night for someone like you."

Ruth gave directions, as we drove down the dark streets leading out of the city and towards the township. I dropped her off at her house and set off back, the headlights shining a path through the darkness, as I drove along the rough roads, swerving to avoid potholes and sometimes groups of people walking along in the warm night. There were no footpaths and it was hard to see people until they loomed close in the car's lights. I took a left turn, then a right, trying to follow the way I had come with Ruth earlier, but after a few minutes I still didn't recognise anything. I came to a dead end and turned the van to return, looking for familiar landmarks. The road had taken me down by a rail yard, where goods were unloaded. I was lost.

I turned again and went back the way I had come, but it was darker now and impossible to see the junctions until I was almost on them.

My palms were sweating, as I found myself back again by the railway, when, suddenly, I came upon three dark, moving shapes in the road. As the headlights flooded them with dazzling light, I could see that two men were kicking and punching a third, who lay curled up in the road, his hands trying to protect his head. I came to a stop, flashed the headlights and sounded the horn, a long blast. The sound exploded into the still night and the two men doing the kicking jumped back and ran off into the darkness. The figure on the ground, who was just a boy, groaned and got to his knees slowly, holding his head.

I opened the car window and called out to him, "Are you okay? Do you need help? Can I take you to the hospital?" As he turned to face me, I was astonished when he called out "Is that you Ba Wendy?" It was a boy I recognised from the township, who was being sponsored by Ruth.

"My God, what is going on here?"

He stumbled slowly to his feet and moved towards the car..

I opened the door for him to get in, but he shook his head.

"No, no, I am okay, I don't need to go to hospital Wendy, you know what that place is like." And indeed I did know, the local hospital was truly a dreadful place.

"I'm visiting my dad. He lives just near here. You need to go now, it's not safe here for you. I will be alright now. You came before they had time to really hurt me. Thank you, thank you. I want to go now." He is getting ready to bolt.

"You must get someone to look at your injuries tonight and make sure you are alright. Ask your dad, when you see him. Go and see a doctor tomorrow."

"Ok I will, but you need to get out of here now. Do you know the way?"

"I will find it. You get inside your dad's house quickly now." I put the car in gear and accelerated away, adrenalin flowing. After a few minutes I came to a main road and managed to find my way from there. I had never been so relieved to get back to the safety of the guest house. I tooted for the watchman to open the gate and drove into the car park. Alan was hovering anxiously, waiting for me and soon I was sitting on the bed with a large gin and tonic, telling him all about It. The room felt so safe and comfortable, despite the dim light and lumpy bed and I was truly grateful to be back. I woke in the night, worrying about the boy I saw earlier, but there was nothing more I could do until morning.

I was up early. I met Ruth and we went together to see the district welfare boss in his scruffy office. The whole building was in an advanced state of dilapidation. Ruth wanted to talk to him about her orphan children and I brought up the problem of street kids and the boy from last night. He seemed an ineffectual man, talkative and disinterested in what we had to say and we didn't get anywhere with him.

We returned to Ruth's place where she looked after 35 children in all. Some were staying with her and a few were fostered. There were several children there today. A dear little baby 'Precious' who smiled at me. Some of the others were frightened of my white face and call me 'Mzungu', a derogatory term for white people. It was uncomfortable to feel so conspicuous and it made me only too aware of the harmful legacy left behind by some of the white people who had previously colonised Zambia. But there wasn't too much time to brood on that.

Later
This has been a day of vivid experiences and here I am at 2 am, with a head full of ideas and heart overflowing. Sleep is far away and it will be light in 4 hours. The watchman is coughing outside, just a yard away, in the darkness. Soon it will be time to start another day.

The next day, Ruth had asked us to lead a workshop on working with troubled children, at her place. She had a pleasant house, in the old part of the town, with an established garden at the back and plenty of trees around. Sixteen people turned up and Ruth had organised things very well. Everyone got a meal and drinks during the day and she was able to translate for those who did not understand English well. The things that children need to thrive are remarkably similar between different countries and cultures, so we felt on familiar ground. We were impressed by Ruth's grasp of all the issues involved, but troubled by the plight of the children she is trying to help. A woman arrived later, with a one-year-old child, severely malnourished and crying with hunger. She looked so pathetic. She was abandoned by her family after her mother died. Ruth gave the woman soya and sugar and advice on what to do. She will go the transient home for orphans tomorrow.

Chapter 5

Returning home – starting a group of supporters for Zambia

Lusaka November 1997
I wiped the sweat from my face and neck, hoping that the rain would come today. The sky was heavy with rainclouds, threatening thunder. The clouds were giants, towering over us, while the earth cowered, below. The garden was parched, the dogs lying panting under the roof, and I felt irritable and exhausted. I sank down into a chair with a drink, which was cold just a minute ago, but now felt lukewarm, the glass sticky and clammy. Everyone was waiting for the storm to break, bringing the start of the rainy season. This was a hard time of year in Zambia, at the end of the long months without rain, when the grasses were parched and shrivelled in the heat, dust blowing everywhere, the animals hungry and desperate for water. The temperature had been rising steadily and the heat was menacing now, as the earth waited, gasping for rain. Maybe today would be the day. I could smell the rain.

I stepped off the veranda and my spirits lifted, as the first heavy drops began to hit the dust. Soon rain was falling, and curtains of water moved across the garden on the warm wind, bending the branches of trees, flattening the grass and lifting the soil. I breathed in the smells, kicked off my shoes and ran out onto the grass. It felt like buckets of water thrown from above that soaked my clothes and streamed off my hair, face and body. I could almost hear the plants drinking in the water. Within hours, green shoots would appear from the ground. This felt so good – the first rain of the season, longed for and transformative. Soon everything would be growing abundantly again, bursting from the ground and advancing with unbelievable speed, like the plants in one of those speeded up wildlife films. People who had land would be busy preparing it for planting, the rivers and water holes would fill up and the roads would be flooded within days; here everything seems to run to extremes: the dry season, followed by the rainy season, no half measures. For a woman like me, raised in a land of pastel colours, gentle rains, gradual changes of season and the long summer hours of dawn and dusk, this was strange, awesome and exhilarating.

It was November when we returned home, at the end of our first year in Zambia, to our house in Cheshire in the UK. Our contract with the Sisters was at an end and we had no idea, at this time, that we would be setting up a charity to work there in the future. Coming home was quite a culture shock; everything was different, and I remember that it seemed so dark. We wondered if our eyes had been affected in some way because we struggled to see when driving or walking in the woods, near to where we lived. We had the lights on at home most of the time. Such a contrast from Zambia, where it was the hottest time of the year.

Although it was wonderful in many ways to be back home in England with friends and family, we found it hard to fit back into our former way of life. The experience of living and working in Zambia had changed us and made us question everything we had previously taken for granted. My work no longer seemed so satisfying and everything seemed to have changed. Of course, we were the ones who had really changed and it was deeply unsettling.

I went back to my former job and tried to settle into the role I had vacated twelve months earlier, but there were problems with that. Things had moved on and I had not been part of it, but had been living in another world, with different priorities. It was hard to change overnight and to engage with the issues which were important to people here. Some of them seemed less vital to me than they had before. None of the families we knew were starving or destitute, even though, of course, they had problems which were vitally important to them and to their children.

Going shopping back in the UK was another thing that was quite a shock to the system. A trip to the supermarket was a bewildering experience at first, with twenty or thirty different varieties of nearly everything you could imagine, on the shelves.

In many parts of Zambia, even in Lusaka, at that time in the 1990s, many foods or other commodities were not available in the shops. I remember that detergent was hard to get, for example and we washed the dishes with soap. It was quite a challenge to source things and, for a while, when we were living in the Northern Province, we existed mainly on rice, onions and tomatoes. But, we got used to it and shopping at the local markets could become quite exciting, when a stall or shopkeeper had something unusual, like meat, or pasta. The word would go round and people like us would rush to buy exotic stuff like dried pasta!

But here we were now, back home in Cheshire, with a cornucopia of foods and goods available to us. We felt privileged and grateful of course, but also a bit confused and disorientated. We didn't quite fit in. Alan had given up his job before moving to Zambia and was looking for work, which was not easy for him. Our lives had changed for ever.

After a few months, we decided to move again. We had family and grandchildren in Devon, where we had spent quite a lot of time, before going to Zambia. Our grandchildren were very young, and we really wanted to see more of them and to be involved in their lives, like most grandparents do, I suppose. We felt that now was the time to seize this opportunity, while we were still young enough to find work. Within a year we had moved and were fortunate to land, by chance, in a busy village community, a place where people were interested in the problems of orphan children in Zambia and willing to help us. We soon got together with them.

The death of our friend and what happened after.

The plight of the little children looked after by Ruth, in Zambia, was something we could not forget and it was this which prompted us, more than anything, to begin fundraising, to send money to support Ruth and her little ones. We still had loyal friends back in Cheshire too, who continued to support us generously for many years.

After an eventful visit to Zambia, early in 2000, as described in the previous chapter, we were even more determined to do what we could to support Ruth and her children. We set to work on fundraising with increased energy.

Sadly, things began to go badly for Ruth later in the year: she became very sick, and when she came to see us in Devon later, she was really too ill to travel. Looking back, I feel certain it was only her fierce determination to ensure that someone would carry on supporting her work with children that propelled her here and onward, to see her friend, Outi Puttonen, in Finland. But her condition deteriorated rapidly and Ruth, brave and inspiring and talented, passed away at the end of the year. This was a terrible blow for her children, for her own family and for the whole community and we felt desperately sad for the passing of our friend, in the prime of her life. We learned too late about the reality of her illness, which she never spoke about, like so many in Zambia at this time.

Dr Outi Puttonen
At this point I want to introduce Dr Outi Puttonen, who, from the very beginning has been a partner with us in supporting, first Ruth and her children and later, the work we established in Zambia. Outi is a Finnish doctor, who was working as a volunteer in Ndola, Zambia in 1997-8, when she first met Ruth. They worked together at a centre for the prevention and treatment of AIDS

and when Outi's parents came from Finland to see her, they met Ruth and visited the home, where she was caring for orphan children. When they returned to Finland, they continued to send funds to support Ruth and her work in Zambia. Eventually they set up a very successful shop selling second hand clothes and other goods. This has been a mainstay of support for the work in Zambia, which continues faithfully, to this day.

When Ruth became sick Outi tried to get medical help and treatment for her, in Finland but, at this time, few treatments were available. Her condition deteriorated very rapidly, when she returned to Zambia and, sadly, Ruth passed away a few weeks later.

Outi was equally as dismayed by Ruth's passing as we were, and she and Alan and I arranged to meet in Helsinki early in 2001, to talk things over and see what we could do. A member of Ruth's family in Ndola had offered to look after her orphan children and had asked for our help to support him but we knew little about the situation. We decided to go to Zambia to see how things were. A few weeks later, Outi and I met at Heathrow airport and travelled out together, wondering what we might find when we arrived in Ndola. When we got to Lusaka, we stayed a few days with the Sisters, before going by bus to the Copperbelt. The Sisters in the community in Lusaka were always so helpful and supportive and it was good to rest after a long flight and catch up with them before going on by bus to other parts of the country.

I hated these bus journeys, which were long, uncomfortable and hot, on roads full of potholes and subject to many unexpected delays. The best way to survive them, I found, was to take an interest in everything and everyone and to write down my observations later. I'm glad now that I did.

From my diary

We got to Lusaka bus station early, but it was already chaotic, crowded with people and vehicles. Buses reversing, giving out clouds of noxious fumes, horns blaring, conductors shouting, touting for business. The bus did not leave until every seat was taken. There is usually a choice of buses going to Ndola but it is impossible to tell which one will leave first. Every conductor claims that theirs will be leaving very soon, in just five minutes! In the end we waited in our seats for an hour before finally setting off through heavy traffic. As usual, a preacher got on and started to harangue us with loud protestations about the need to repent and to find Jesus and, crucially, to support his mission! He walked up and down for the first hour or two, shouting his message.

At home in the UK he would be heckled or even ejected by exasperated passengers, but here people are very patient and polite and he continued walking up and down until we stopped at Kabwe – about two hours. In competition with the voice of the preacher, was the film being shown on the screens. Today it featured Pierce Brosnan and some other soft voiced Irishmen and was set in the rural west of Ireland. I found it hard to make out what they were saying and the action seemed to be in the semi darkness of a rainy landscape. A strange contrast, as we travelled through the bush, in the scorching heat, with stunted trees and tall elephant grass racing past the windows.

When we arrived in Ndola the Sisters very generously offered us accommodation for our stay. Sr Elizabeth, who is a nurse herself and had known and worked with Ruth, always went out of her way to help and advise, as well as offering generous support and hospitality. We would have found it all so much more difficult without her. We spent the week visiting Ruth's relatives and others connected with the proposed home for orphan children, but we were unsure how to proceed and found it difficult to make a proper assessment of the situation in such a short time.

We met with Ruth's relative, Henry, the next day and went with him to a pleasant house where he was living with his wife, his own children and some others. His wife went out of her way to be charming to us and the house and furnishings were immaculate. They gave us a nice lunch and we spent the morning listening to his ideas on what he was planning. It seemed that he wished to set up a small home for children in the town and had already appointed a committee. Outi and family have been sending money to Henry and this provides an income for him, his family and his relatives as well as the orphans. He clearly had no experience of working with vulnerable children and was previously working at a bank.

I spent the evening talking with Outi and a sleepless night thinking about it. Henry did not impress me for some reason, although he had been friendly enough. I was worried that he saw this as an opportunity for himself and his own family, rather than a mission to help the most vulnerable children. On the other hand, he was Ruth's brother, and this must count for something. Was this what we wanted and were we going about it the right way? Was this going to reach the women and children who needed it most? I decided to go and see the Social Welfare manager and to talk to others working in this area.

Before the end of the week, I had contacted various people, including the director of the health education project in the Copperbelt, with whom Alan and I had worked during our first year. He was a very experienced and competent man, with clear ideas on setting and monitoring realistic objectives for working with vulnerable children. I asked if he would be willing for us to approach a worker from his team to act as an advisor for the project we were planning to support and help us to reach the children and families who were most in need.

We went over to Kitwe to talk it over with him and he agreed to help. Hellen Mpundu was still working with his organisation, and she soon volunteered to take it on. I knew that she had been a friend of Ruth and shared many of the ideas that Ruth herself had tried to put into action, in her lifetime. She had a passion for children and for promoting the rights of women. I knew we could work together.

Becoming a registered charity.

When we returned to the UK we were buzzing with ideas, which we discussed with our group and we got started on fund raising activities straight away. We discussed plans to become a registered charity and we drew up a governing document, setting out our principles and main aims. We were very fortunate to be able to appoint a talented and committed group of Trustees and committee members, who had experience and expertise in a range of different areas.

Kelle, the daughter of one of our Trustees designed a beautiful logo for us, which represented the essence of what we stood for. We were delighted with it.

We were officially registered with the UK Charities commission in June 2003. The charity was named 'Families for Children Zambia' and its objectives were as follows;

- To relieve those in need by advancing their education.

- To protect, care for and educate orphans and other vulnerable children, by working with Zambian people and supporting local community initiatives.

- To promote family based care for orphan children by giving support to carers.

We agreed that our regular quarterly grants would be targeted on small community-based projects, which were focused on supporting family based care for orphans and vulnerable children. We decided not to supply large amounts of money at any one time, but make modest donations, allowing projects to develop at their own pace so that they did not become too large or out of touch with the communities they served.

We wanted to encourage people to build up their own strengths and skills and resources to improve their lives, by offering low key support when needed. We would also support some capital projects, which would improve the sustainability of programs in the longer term. We hoped that they would become completely independent of us eventually.

Looking back, I can see that we did very much adhere to these principles, throughout our involvement in Zambia. The fact that we encouraged and empowered people and offered support and resources, rather than direct management was key to understanding how things developed later. We always made it clear that we were there to help people to develop their own solutions to problems in the longer term.

Chapter 6

Kantolomba

Through her previous work, Hellen had identified the township in the Copperbelt which was the one most desperately in need of help. This was Kantolomba, on the outskirts of Ndola. Looking back, I sometimes think how much easier it would have been for us to support a small children's home in the town of Ndola, as Henry had proposed. But somehow Kantolomba was a challenge we could not ignore.

In those early days the compound of Kantolomba was a lawless place. It was some way out of the town and had no services of any kind. It had no school, no clinic, no home based care, no police presence. It was a dangerous and chaotic slum township, frequented by drunks and criminals. It was known for its illegal beer brewing and distilling of spirits, with several taverns and drinking haunts. There was a cemetery which bordered the township and a constant procession of funeral vehicles passed through on its broken and potholed road. There were many single parent or child headed households, sick people and orphans and vulnerable children who desperately needed help, mainly due to the devastation caused by the AIDS pandemic.

This was the situation we found when we arrived there in 2001 and I must admit that I was dismayed when I first saw Kantolomba. We had taken on a tough challenge. I talked it over with Sr Elizabeth who had been in Ndola for some years and who was working in another compound: she confirmed my first impression. Kantolomba was a place where nobody wanted to go but which desperately needed help.

Hellen's early memories of Kantolomba

Most people there were living by illegal means and were wanted by the police for various crimes.. Why did people live there? It was isolated, it was beside a cemetery, which was a bad place to be. They ran there to hide, when they had committed crimes in other places. When the police came, they came armed and sometimes there was shooting. It was an illegal compound, with no electricity and no services of any kind. There was plenty of employment in town but people were not interested in going to work but just in drinking, illegal brewing and dealing drugs. There were many bars and drinking places. They were selling to other communities. They also involved their children in this and there were so many early marriages of girl children. Parents did not take their children to school. People said to me "Don't go there. It is a lawless place. They will kill you". Child labour and child abuse was common. I had to try to change things, to change the way people thought, to make things better for the children.

At first it was hard, people did not trust me and I didn't trust them. They thought I had come from the government or the police, to spy on them, to get them arrested. I started working with a group of women and sometimes, when women came to meetings, they would agree with me and we would plan together, then they would go away and send their children for work or talk against me. Sometimes they would steal from me. It was very disappointing. But I didn't give up. I had to keep on for the sake of the children and slowly people came to understand that education was important for their children.

Hellen went to see the chairman of the community to get a place to meet and an old former tavern was identified as a suitable premises for the school initially, although it was far from ideal. This was when we got involved and eventually we were able to send money to purchase the building and begin to get it established as a community school. There were no other prospective buyers!

When we visited a few months later, Hellen and her group had cleared and brightened up the place as much as they could. It was clean and had a fresh coat of paint and was decorated with toilet paper streamers. There were lots of children milling around, volunteers were helping with cleaning and cooking and five teachers had been appointed. Hellen lived amongst the people and worked alongside them for those early months and had already made a change and an improvement in the lives of the children.

She knew every family and went to visit the households regularly if there were problems within the home. Despite all the odds, she had begun to win the trust of the group of parents who were working with her. Of course, there were always people who were against Hellen and her team and who were protecting their own interests. She had a hard battle to fight. At the time we didn't even realise the full extent of the situation in that lawless community. It was only later that we began to understand it. Kantolomba community school was the first school ever to be set up in that area and that is something to celebrate.

Building Kantolomba

In September 2002 we went with two members of our team, Peter and Amanda, to visit Kantolomba. Peter was a civil engineer and Amanda a social worker and teacher. During our early years in Zambia, Alan and I were very aware that we were lacking many of the skills and knowledge that would be most helpful. We were happy that members of our UK group were keen to visit Zambia and were very lucky to have Peter and Amanda alongside us, especially on the early visits. Peter was an engineer, with extensive experience and we always felt much safer when he was with us; there were few practical things that he could not tackle and his skills were much in demand, wherever he went. He would draw up plans for buildings on the back of an envelope and could see, at a glance, when things were broken or needed maintenance. There were plenty of things needing maintenance wherever we went in Zambia, and Peter always had his bag of tools at hand.

Amanda was very skilled in training and assessment and worked well alongside Alan with this, but she also had a wonderful empathy with people, especially women and children, and the ability to connect with them and understand them on a deeper level. This was invaluable for me, as I was always trying to keep an eye on too many issues at once, plan the next move and maintain some distance. Other members of our UK committee visited with us over the years: they also brought valuable skills and expertise and we came to depend very much on their help.
Our regular debriefing meetings became important for us all and there was much soul searching and laughter, when our well-intentioned plans had gone awry. There were tears as well, sometimes, but everything seems more manageable when it is shared.

My Diary
Today we drove out to the township in a beat-up taxi. The road was almost impassable, with enormous potholes and dried up rain ditches, dust blowing everywhere, and the road flanked by scraps of tattered plastic bags and piles of other rubbish. There was no sign to Kantolomba, but a piece of cardboard at the roadside marked the way to the cemetery. The taxi driver knew the place but looked dubious when we told him we were setting up a school there. I could see Amanda and Peter were not impressed, but they kept their cool, even as we passed the noisy taverns at the entrance to Kantolomba, with drunken men wandering around the road. We finally reached the place, in front

of another tavern, where Henry and some of the teachers were waiting to greet us. Henry was the manager in charge at this stage, but Hellen was living in Kantolomba and doing all the hands on work with the staff and volunteers. Henry, meanwhile, had set up an office in town, where he did all the admin and communicated with me and other donors by email.

As we drove in, Amanda was amazed to see a road being dug through the hillside to make a short-cut to another township. There were gangs of women digging the road by hand, with rough hoes and spades.. Everywhere it was the women who were doing the work, carrying water or wood on their heads, cooking, selling things at the roadside, babies on their backs, out in the boiling sun.

We walked around the area a bit and were dismayed to see so many funerals passing on their way to the cemetery, which was just at the end of the road. One after another, funeral lorries drove slowly by, crowded with people, standing up and singing, to mark the passing of their friend or relative. Amongst the people walking the road were women and children, mainly girls, coming from the fields, or the market, carrying large loads on their heads. Little boys were playing, kicking footballs made from plastic bags, or pulling wire toys, or chasing the goats and piglets around. There didn't seem to be much playtime for the girls, and some were already looking after younger siblings, even quite young children had babies on their backs. This was a dangerous place, especially for women and girls, who were more likely to be accosted by drunken men, of whom there were many. Children were also recruited to go into other townships, to sell illegal liquor, which was brewed in homemade stills in Kantolomba.

Kantolomba in the late 1990s

There were many things we didn't notice on our first visit, but what we discovered made us even more determined to go ahead and, before we left Ndola, we met with officials from the council, to secure the ownership of the former tavern. Peter recalls that there was a form to be filled in at the local government office to formalise this, but when we requested one, we were told they only had one. Eventually we persuaded the council officer to lend us the form, and we had several photocopies made.

Later, after lengthy negotiations, we managed to purchase a piece of land on the opposite side of the road, which could be used to develop another building. The school did still look very much like the original tavern at this stage, but Peter could see the potential. We had already raised some money for improving the school, so we arranged to meet with Henry and his committee, at the office in Ndola, to discuss budgets and to agree on a realistic plan.

We sat around a table at the local hotel in Ndola, which was called the Savoy. It was far from grand, however and had an outdoor pool with the greenest, most stagnant water I have ever seen. Henry and his fellow committee members were disappointed that we could not afford a state-of-the-art new school, for which they had extravagant hopes, far beyond our means to supply. Eventually though, they agreed to compromise and manage with what funds we had. Peter set to work straight away, designing and drawing up plans for the reconstruction of the school and advising on the purchase of materials. The materials available locally were very limited and not always of the best quality, but he did the best he could with what he had and soon came up with a good design.

The rest of us spent time with the teachers, social workers and volunteers. The teachers were mainly young and enthusiastic and there was no shortage of children wanting to come to the school. Education was to be free for all children and no uniform would be required. In addition, the children were to be given food at school whenever possible and their families were to be visited regularly. There were many households headed by elderly grandmothers or older children, who desperately needed help and support.

The school is established

Changes

After the first years, Hellen left the Copperbelt, for a high-profile job in Lusaka, working with the Zambian community schools' secretariat. We were very disappointed to see her leave but Hellen had already established the main principles of working with the poorest families and encouraging women and children to improve their lives through education. Without her influence and determination, this would not have happened in the same way.

From this time onward we visited Zambia as often as possible, at least once or twice a year, but we were dependent on the leaders and staff of the projects to get on and do things their own way. We gave them our trust and respect, but we could not know the day-to-day details of how things unfolded. We spent time every visit with teams in agreeing and reviewing objectives and monitoring accounts and finances, but in the end a great deal was based on mutual trust and a shared commitment to helping vulnerable children and families. There were inevitably going to be some misunderstandings and miscommunication.

For a long time, for example, we did not understand why Hellen left Kantolomba, the project which she had started and put so much of herself into. We were sad to see her go, but it was not until very much later that she told me how difficult things had been between herself, as the co-ordinator of the project, and Henry, the manager. They had very different ideas about the objectives and programs they each wanted to develop. Eventually the disagreement between them was such that it became impossible to work together. Most of this was not communicated to us at the time, so we were left to speculate and to continue to support the work in Kantolomba as best we could. Hellen has told me since that she did try to inform us about the situation, but, since Henry was the one sending all the emails and reports, and we only saw Hellen for a few days a year, we didn't get the message.

Chapter 7

Development of work in Kantolomba

Renovation of the school was well under way when we next saw Kantolomba, and the area was covered in piles of bricks and other materials. There was only one useable classroom, but the teachers were doing a good job and many lessons were taken outside. It was hard not to be distracted by the piglets and goats and chickens running around but the children and teachers took all this in their stride.

I enjoyed watching an impromptu football game, in a field of rough grass, in the boiling heat. There appeared to be few rules, but much enthusiasm, with players chasing around after the ball. Most of the children were barefoot. Every so often the ball disappeared into the long grass, followed by a small crowd of shouting children. The field was lined with supporters and there was much dancing and singing and cheering on the sidelines when a goal was scored.

It was fun to watch the children and teachers enjoying themselves and we were completely drawn into the spirit of it all. Our hard-working days were lightened by occasions like this and soon we were singing and jumping about on the side-lines like fools, not sure who we were supporting, or even which team was which. There was a teacher with a whistle, which he seemed to be blowing most of the time, but I don't think anyone took much notice and the game surged on, unchecked.

Things now began to move at a faster pace and when we visited in December 2003, the school buildings were almost completed. We were introduced to the new project social worker and co-ordinator, a young woman called Gina, who was pleasant and friendly and good with the children and staff alike. We found her easy to work with and were happy with this new appointment, although I personally very much regretted the loss of Hellen Mpundu.

From my diary
We drove into Kantolomba in a minibus, after collecting drinks and snacks for the children. The School looked better than any of us expected and we were really pleased. It looked almost finished, with desks in place, a few posters hanging at crooked angles on the walls, the grounds cleaned and tidied. We got a great reception from the children – about 250 of them – and staff and volunteers, with singing and dancing and drumming. My son Michael was with us and he joined in with the drumming, while Amanda danced with the children and Peter was busy, measuring, filming and looking at all the buildings. Alan and I were quite overcome by the welcome. There were speeches and more dancing and singing before we left.

We enjoyed this wonderful welcome, but we also wanted to look below the surface and try to assess what had been achieved in the past year. Peter, our project engineer, was keen to see how the building was progressing and to help with practical details and planning the next stage. We also wanted to see how effective the teaching had been and how the community had benefitted, so decided to attempt an evaluation. This involved talking with children, carers, teachers, volunteers and community members, and for this we needed to recruit someone to translate. We planned to take pictures and make a short video, to illustrate the life of a family living in Kantolomba' which we could show to our supporters and potential donors.

On the next day we recruited a young local woman, Mary, to act as our interpreter, since none of us could speak Bemba and most of the children had only a scant knowledge of English. We had hoped to remain as inconspicuous as possible while visiting families in the township, but we should have known better. Everywhere we went we were followed by groups of giggling children. Mary, who was interpreting for us, was strikingly beautiful, so we also had to contend with frequent attention from drunken men, who fancied themselves, and young boys who hung around hoping to be noticed.

We visited the home of one of the children from the school, whose mother had agreed for us to do so. The child's name was Sarah, and she lived with her mum and brother and sister in a small mud brick house of one room, divided by a curtain. Her mum also had a small baby, which was on her back all the time and looked thin and fretful. I was dismayed to see the conditions they lived in and how poor they were. Sarah slept on the floor on a blanket, which was her treasured possession. Some of the children had no blanket of their own. Her breakfast consisted of a cup of water and a piece of bread when there was any available. Before going to school, Sarah had chores to do, such as fetching water and sweeping the floor and minding the baby.

She loved school, where she was given a meal every day, but she could not always attend. We were told that she and her sister had only one suitable dress between them, so had to take turns to wear this to school. We found this heart-breaking and reported back to the project social worker, who promised to visit the family and to make sure that Sarah and her sister at least had suitable clothes to wear. But the problems faced by Sarah's family were common to so many in Kantolomba and other townships, where people had lost family members and had no breadwinner. We could not hope to reach them all. It was overwhelming to think of the enormity of the problems and sometimes we felt despairing. Surely the small amount we could offer was just a drop in the ocean of need? We tried to overcome this feeling by concentrating on the limited objectives we had set ourselves and were sustained by something one of the Sisters told us. "It is better to light a candle than to curse the darkness". My mother, a Yorkshire woman, would have put it another way. "A little help is worth a lot of pity".

Our assessment revealed what the project staff already knew: the poorest carers in Kantolomba were still struggling to survive, even though their children were attending school. After talking with the team, we suggested that they start an emergency 'Hardship Fund', to help those most in need. This would be a system of small loans, to enable people to set up small business ventures, for income generation. We hoped that the fund would be able to help with things such as shoes, clothes, blankets and some basic foods, to enable families to survive. There was already a fund such as this in one of the other compounds we knew in Lusaka. It was administered by a group of local people, who met regularly to determine those in the greatest need, and it worked very well.

It was difficult to give to people directly, as they were jealous of any favour shown to their neighbours. Volunteers who came to Zambia with us were sometimes keen to share whatever they had, on the spot, even to the point of taking the shirt off their backs. But this was a mistake and caused problems for the project team after we left.

Maybe we did not always give as much thought as we could have done about the best way to support people, sometimes favouring those who came to our notice over those who did not. But how could it be otherwise? It was so difficult to have any kind of honest relationships, when we were always, inevitably, seen as rich donors. We were far from rich, of course and made sure that we stayed in the cheapest accommodation and used local buses when in Zambia, but this was luxurious to someone living in Kantolomba.

There was also the colonial history of Zambia, which surely had an influence on how we were seen by local people. Maybe I was too sensitive about this. I asked Ruth about it once and she replied that her people had been in that part of Africa for millennia, while the British had been there less than a hundred years. Their influence was merely a scratch on the surface and would soon be all but forgotten. I hoped that this was true and found the thought strangely comforting.

Volunteers at Kantolomba

One of the things which we always found heart-warming when we visited Kantolomba was meeting with the volunteers who worked at the school. These were local people, mostly women, who helped with various tasks such as preparing vegetables, cooking, serving meals, sewing, woodwork and maintenance around the place. The volunteers who prepared and served meals were a lively and supportive group, who knew everything that was going on in the township and kept an eye on families who were struggling to survive.

When they came to the school, they enjoyed wearing a kind of 'uniform' of T shirts and aprons, which identified them as a group. They made the aprons themselves, of course, but the shirts were bought with project funds and they were very proud of them. This group of women always gave us a great welcome when we visited and we enjoyed their traditional singing and dancing. They worked hard preparing vast quantities of mealie meal porridge, called Nshima, for the children's midday meal and the vegetable stew which went with it. Sometimes they added groundnuts to the stew, for protein, and occasionally there would be meat or chicken, or fish, for a special occasion.

I preferred the vegetables, as the meat was always tough and the fish full of bones. Alan and I usually ate with the staff and volunteers when at Kantolomba, but we were not very good at eating with our fingers, in the traditional way and got ourselves really messy in the process. Thank goodness they were scrupulous about hand washing and there was always soap and water nearby. The children washed their hands at the tap in the school yard, before coming in to eat and again afterwards, but they all managed very well, even the little ones, and avoided getting food up to their elbows, like Alan and me!

The women were used to hard physical work and were much stronger than any of us. They delighted in showing us how they stirred a giant pot of Nshima over a charcoal fire, to feed several hundred children. Alan had a go, but soon discovered it was really hard work and the women found this very funny.

Volunteers at Kantolomba

Alan stirring the pot

Work with the Teachers

Early in 2004, my son Michael, an experienced teacher, who had been with us in Zambia on our previous visit, took a sabbatical from work and went to stay in Ndola for 3 months to work with the teachers at Kantolomba. He accomplished a great deal in a short time, by putting in long hours at the school. His influence was felt long after he left and things improved considerably. Here are some extracts from his report dated June 2004.

The teachers do an amazing job, considering their own difficult financial circumstances and the challenges they face every day at school. Simple compassion and a determination to combat the effects of poverty are what motivate the teachers at Kantolomba school to turn up immaculately dressed every morning, plan lessons, teach tirelessly and know all the names and most of the stories of their pupils...

Training. Not all the teachers at the school have received primary training and those that have do remarkably well with a fairly sketchy grounding. They were all keen to discuss new ideas and possible solutions to classroom problems – differentiation, motivation, planning, use of resources and so on. My approach was to offer advice and leave it to the teachers to decide what they wanted to use and what to leave aside, depending on their styles and strengths.

Teenage girls in particular start to drop out around the age of 14 onwards. Children dropping out at this stage never get the chance to see if they could pass the exams to continue past grade 8 into secondary education. Most families have elderly or ill members at home or young children and these girls are the first in line to stay home as carers. Another factor is early marriages for girls. Children also stay home to help with income generation or because they are too hungry or ill to come in or even because they may be sharing clothes with a brother or sister. On the days when lunch is provided, school attendance is high, so providing a meal every day should have a big impact on pupil progress.

Creative activities. After consultation with the teachers, we decided to introduce more activities into the curriculum and purchased some materials for crafts, painting, mime and drama and creative development and wall displays. We also began some sport and games. The teachers were all keen to attend during their holidays, to learn simple group games and sports, including how to referee. We bought a bag of sports resources and PE was written into the curriculum.

A Saturday morning sport and talk group was begun with the newly appointed HIV/ AIDS awareness coordinator. A nearby field was cleared by the group of young men, who then met on Saturday mornings to play football and rounders for a couple of hours, before returning to the classroom to discuss HIV and sexual behaviour. This group was very successful and well attended. A new football team was subsequently set up for young men aged 18 – 25 and some coaching arranged to bring them on. The whole initiative began to address the issue of young and sexually active young men who are often left out or opt out of HIV awareness schemes. The negative face of this is that it exacerbates men's sense of disempowerment, already huge, due to job losses and traditional family and community roles. This loss of self-esteem can lead to alcoholism and risky sexual behaviour.

In conclusion, the teachers at Kantolomba school started in one room in a derelict tavern and, with very little in the way of resources, they are now getting amazing results with the pupils. They are very dedicated and professional in their approach. I hope that, in 2 years time, there will be a group of pupils who have gone through to secondary level, with access to higher grades and further education. In order to do this, space for another class will have to be found, together with more staff and resources. With support, this can happen.

Michael's time spent with the teachers was a most helpful and influential intervention at this crucial stage and he did a good job, cycling the few miles to the school every day, one of the first to arrive in the mornings and one of the last to leave. He worked hard and professionally and made good relationships with the teachers. They all seemed to benefit very much from what they learned from him and so did the children.

When we visited Kantolomba, the following year, things were much improved, with the school now rebuilt and refurbished and about 250 children attending every day. The standard of education enjoyed by the children had improved dramatically, and we found them full of confidence and new skills. Their morale was high, and the classroom walls were covered with colourful posters, charts and drawings. We spent an enjoyable morning watching the children and teachers playing netball, football and other games they had improvised, and which involved fishing nets, balls, bats, bells and whistles!

The project staff were proud to report that some adult students had been learning home craft skills, including tailoring. A carpentry school was starting to help some of the young men to learn woodworking skills and the hardship fund was doing quite well, with some recipients (mainly elderly grandmothers and widows) engaging in small business ventures. We bought fritters from one of the women, who had set up a stall near the school. The fritters, made of some kind of batter, fried in sunflower oil, were greasy and bland, to my palate, but seemed to be popular with people walking back from attending funerals. We ate them anyway!

The manager, Henry, was making progress in sourcing funds from organisations within Zambia, which were intended to support some of the poorest households, especially child headed households, with essentials such as mealie meal, beans, soap, salt and cooking oil.

By this time there were hundreds of children attending or waiting to attend the school and there was an urgent need for more space. Peter, our project engineer, had already drawn up plans for the development of the site opposite the school and we managed to get a grant from a trust within Zambia to build extra classrooms and outbuildings. Peter was consulting with the team on the detail of how the building was to proceed. Work had begun on clearing the land and building a boundary wall, with the help of volunteers from the community. We were happy to see there had been many other initiatives at Kantolomba, which had improved the lives of all involved with the project, from the teachers and other staff to the children, families, volunteers and carers. The school and centre seemed to be an oasis in a neglected and deprived area and we were hopeful that it would begin to drive more development in the township. All this had taken some intensive work in Zambia and fundraising on the home front as well.

Looking back on all this now, twenty years later, I often wonder how things might have developed if this very positive progress had continued, but there were many obstacles in the way and problems which we had not anticipated. We tried always to agree aims and common ground rules with the managers of the projects we supported and to trust them to get on with it, allowing flexibility for them to respond to crises or opportunities. This worked well with Hellen Mpundu, who was strong, committed and determined, but maybe it was not so successful with others. We had some hard lessons to learn.

But, in the meantime, Kantolomba school was doing well.

Looking good with new desks

Chapter 8

Umwana Kasembe Freedom Compound Chilanga

After leaving Kantolomba, Hellen took up a job with the Zambian Community Schools Secretariat, a prestigious organisation, with links to other organisations throughout Africa. At that time Zambia was in the forefront of the movement to establish community schools and Hellen was recruited because of her experience in this area. She was a passionate and committed speaker and was called upon to speak eloquently at various conferences and meetings. However, she found, after a while, that the work did not suit her: She missed working directly with women and children in the poorest communities. This was her real vocation and she wanted to get back to living amongst the people.

She chose Chilanga, just south of Lusaka, as a place to live and work and soon she managed to acquire a house and a piece of land there. She was helped in this by her eldest son, Musonda, who was already skilled in building and carpentry. She had been able to save, while employed by the Secretariat and used her own money to get started. Her target area was called Freedom compound and was just across the road from where she set up her home and centre for women and children, which she called Umwana Kasembe.

During these years at Umwana Kasembe, Hellen kept in contact with the team in Kantolomba and met quite regularly with some of the teachers, when she was visiting family in the Copperbelt. She also sent them money, from the funds she had saved, while working for the Secretariat. She told me that Kantolomba was never far from her thoughts and she did what she could to help the people there. But in the meantime, there were many problems in Freedom compound, in Chilanga, which occupied her.

This was where Hellen had chosen to work and, as I might have guessed, it was one of the toughest areas. The nearby compound, had high levels of child abuse, AIDS and violence against women. It was an overcrowded area, with few open spaces or gardens and it was normal for at least 10 families to share one pit latrine. Polygamy was common and men expected their women to remain at home, care for the household and do most of the work. There were many early marriages and little prospect of education or advancement for girls. The main employer locally was Chilanga Cement, and the area was often polluted with cement dust when the wind was in a certain direction.

From my diary
I got a lift into Lusaka in an old battered truck and met Hellen by the post office. We walked through Soweto market to the bus stop. There were stalls selling everything, all jumbled together; meat stalls with indescribable piles of offal, cows feet and tails, heads, ears and tongues. Nothing is wasted. Piles of flesh and bones. Flies everywhere! We got onto the minibus, which was very hot and crowded, and headed south down the Kafue road. Out of the city and through fields of red earth and newly planted crops, to Chilanga, where Hellen stays. Her small house is just a short walk from the road. Just across from Freedom township, which is very poor and semi derelict. We sat under a tree, talking about the project she has set up, called Umwana Kasembe, in the Bemba language, which is her native tongue. She translates it as something like, "Your child is an axe, which you cannot abandon, even if it hurts you". What she wants to create is a kind of refuge, a safe house, a therapeutic place for children. She has a schoolroom, and two small rooms children can sleep in. She gave me Nshima and cows feet for lunch!

Hellen told me that the early days at Umwana Kasembe were very difficult. She had a lot of opposition from the men in the community, both because she was a woman and because she was from a different tribe than most of the people who lived in the compound. They refused to allow her to use any premises there and resorted to underhand measures to try to discredit her. When she used her own home to set up a small classroom for pre-school children, a man from the community reported her to the district council. But when someone from the Council actually paid a visit, he was very impressed with what he saw.

In an early report from Umwana Kasembe, Hellen described her work with families and vulnerable children, in these words:
Fostering starts early, as some girls get married at fifteen or sixteen and then take on the task of looking after family members in their house, before they have their own children. Most families start with fostering their own relatives. In our programme, ten families are fostering, and we try to provide a family package. By this we mean, encouraging them to understand the things that are needed for children to grow up into responsible people. We are providing them with essentials like food and schooling. These families have a total of 55 children and the youngest is 18 months. The total number of children we are supporting has increased to 140, including the children we support to go to government schools.

Grandma with children Umwana Kasembe

Hellen and her women volunteers who are working in Freedom compound have a very tough job, as the area is desperately poor. When we visited, we were impressed by the work being done with the 'fostering families' which are mainly headed by widows, grandparents, or even older children. We met some of these families, who would hardly survive without the practical and emotional support given to them by the volunteers from Umwana Kasembe project.

We found that some of the older children were searching the piles of rubbish along the roadside looking for items they could use or sell. There is a busy main road alongside the compound and sometimes things are thrown out by truck drivers heading south towards Kafue or Livingstone. We met one boy who was being looked after by his uncle, who was unable to earn a living because he was totally blind. The boy told us that Hellen and her son Musonda had shown him how to make jewellery and other items which he hoped to sell at the craft markets in Lusaka.

Some of the men in the township were still trying to prevent their wives from taking part in activities organised at Hellen's project, but she held out, encouraging and supporting the women, and slowly things began to take shape. Hellen always believed in the importance of gardening and growing useful plants for food and she gave some of the women small plots of land to cultivate, to help to feed their families. This was something that our dear friend, Ruth, who you met in a previous chapter, would have been pleased to see and we were pleased too. Hellen also taught tailoring, tie and dye, jewellery making and other skills to help people to earn a living.

Hellen told me that she tried to be a role model for the women, encouraging them to become stronger and more assertive, in standing up for their human rights. When she first arrived in Chilanga it was common for women to be beaten and abused by their husbands, but she encouraged them to report to the Umwana Kasembe project and seek help from there, both for themselves and for their children. She set up a small 'Safe House' to accommodate a few people on a temporary basis, and worked with the police victim support group, to help protect women and children.

Over the years, things did improve, especially after the law was changed to protect widows from 'property grabbing' by their late husband's relatives. This practice, which Alan and I had learned about when we were working with the police, in our first year in Zambia, was a corruption from the traditional custom, which was intended to support the children. Instead, greedy relatives would often descend on the poor widow and grab all her worldly goods, without even taking on the care of the children. Or sometimes they would take the children too, leaving their mother alone and penniless. The police in the victim support groups had previously told us about this and the difficulties they had in dealing with it, especially in rural areas.

There were many orphan children, in Freedom Township, who had been taken on by relatives, sometimes reluctantly. It was painfully clear that some of these children were suffering in different ways. Women did most of the work as well as the childcare and had little power to change things. Mistaken and harmful beliefs about so called cures for AIDS made the situation worse. The belief that AIDS could be cured by having sex with a young child, a virgin, was prevalent, for example. Hellen's attempts to help the women to challenge their situation caused anger from some of the men, who tried their best to undermine and sabotage her work.

When we visited with a volunteer Liz, who is a doctor from the UK, she was distressed to find clear evidence of abuse and neglect in the children she saw but felt powerless to do anything other than to identify and diagnose and report to project staff. There was no further action she could take, at this time. Hellen later told us that she encouraged and supported families to report to the police, if their child was abused, but this was not always successful. Often the charge was dropped, with the accused paying a bribe to the police not to prosecute.

One of Hellen's major achievements over the years was to raise awareness of issues such as early marriages, child labour and sexual abuse of women and children. We were able to help sometimes, by organising training in child protection for both community members and police. This was well attended and we developed good training materials which we left in Zambia, to be used by others. But it was Hellen's determination to fight for the rights of women and children that was the biggest factor in improving the situation in Chilanga.

Musonda. An unsung Hero.

I would like to say something here about Musonda, Hellen's eldest son.. He has worked alongside his mother throughout the time we have known her and has been a tremendous support and help. He has many skills: building and carpentry, brick making, farming and working with vulnerable young people. One of his skills is in managing projects and he is a talented entrepreneur. Without his help, we would have struggled to accomplish many of the challenges we took on, alongside Hellen. He has found creative ways to raise funds and has supervised all building works at Umwana Kasembe. He combined the final year of his degree in business studies, which we helped to fund, with hands on management of projects in Chilanga. He has enabled several young people there to learn carpentry, building and other skills, and encouraged them to become independent, and earn their own living.

Hellen and Musonda have always emphasised the importance of growing vegetables to provide fresh food. In 2008 we managed to raise the funds for a borehole to be sunk and we saw very encouraging developments the next time we visited, the following year.

From my diary.
Our first impression, when we arrived, was of vegetables and flowers growing everywhere. Some of the older children were making a garden, and women volunteers were tending the vegetables, washing clothes and cleaning the classrooms. We saw tomatoes, sweet potatoes, maize, okra, pumpkin leaves, groundnuts, and cassava growing and we were so pleased to learn that the vegetables are being used to supplement the food given to the children each day. Now that the team has a secure water supply, their morale has received an enormous boost. Some of the volunteers were busy making tie and dye materials,

and jewellery. They showed them to us with pride and we bought some of the materials to take home and sell in the UK. Every day, members of the community can come, and wash blankets and clothes and the kids play with water. The women volunteers and parents regularly help in the garden and have made a duty rota for each week. Some households are given seeds to grow vegetables in their own kitchen gardens. They tell us. "Water is life - every morning we see green vegetables".

We were not there when the drilling for the borehole finally reached water but Hellen described it to us. Apparently, there was a fountain of water gushing everywhere and people were cheering and standing underneath, the children running around and shouting, getting soaked. I wish we could have seen it. Hellen phoned me on that day to tell me about it and I could hear the excitement in her voice and the cheering in the background.

While Hellen was working on gardening and nutrition, Musonda had been busy training a group of boys to be self-sufficient in different ways. Some of them had formerly been street kids, with no families and they were offered a temporary home in one of the houses. Musonda kept an eye on their welfare and taught them skills in carpentry and building, which would enable them to find employment locally. All of them did so eventually.

Woodwork class

Chapter 9

Volunteering in Zambia

We had no paid staff in the UK working for our charity so, in a sense, everyone was a volunteer and had an important part to play. We would not have got far without our committee, Trustees, treasurer and fundraisers who were the mainstay of the organisation and kept us going through many difficulties. Alongside the positive times, the planning and talking about progress, there were also times when there was bad news to share from Zambia and we really needed to support each other, stay resolute and find a way forward. Those of us who were able to go to Zambia were fortunate, and we felt privileged to do so but, understandably, it was not for everyone.

When the charity became well known in our local area here in Devon, we began to receive offers of help from people who were keen to visit the country. Some of these people were mature professionals: doctors, engineers, accountants, teachers, carpenters, electricians who had a great deal of expertise and experience to offer. Others were younger, but keen and committed. We soon decided we needed a clear policy on how to select people and to prepare them for going to Zambia. We wanted to make sure that potential volunteers were resourceful and able to take care of themselves. Maybe we should devise some kind of practical task or experience which would give them an opportunity to show what they were made of? Or this was the intention anyway.

My diary
"Whose stupid idea was this?" Alan said, as we battled our way through the cold wind and rain across the wilds of Dartmoor.

"Well it seemed like a good one at the time."

"This is absolutely nothing like Zambia – exactly the opposite in fact. Oh, damn it, I've got a boot full of water. Can you even see the place yet?"

"No – can you?"

"I think it's down there at the bottom of the hill – that kind of barn place, by the trees. I wonder if the others have found it yet?"

"I hope not, we were supposed to be there first. Just remind me why we are doing this, can you? Something to do with resilience and adaptability wasn't it? Feels more like endurance to me!"

"Oh come on, what's the matter with you? We're not even there yet!"

"Here we are," Peter said, as we arrived at our destination, a rough cottage, with walls, a door, roof and windows and nothing much else. "Welcome to our luxury weekend hideaway." He opened the door and ushered us, wet and muddy, inside. It didn't look very inviting but at least it was dry. A bare room, with a stone floor, sparsely furnished with a table and a few chairs, an old settee, a big fireplace with candles on the mantlepiece. There was a sink and a camping gas stove. It smelled of wood and damp and the small windows reminded me of my grandad's cottage in Derbyshire. At least that had an outside toilet. Here there was just a spade and a loo roll.

"Plenty of wood in the barn," Peter said, "let's get the fire going." He and Alan went outside to get logs, while Amanda sorted out the cupboard and put away the food she'd brought. I headed upstairs to explore the bedrooms which were freezing but had mattresses on the floor, so I dumped my rucksack and put out my sleeping bag.

Over the next hour or so the other prospective volunteers arrived, having parked their cars a mile or so away. There is no access to the cottage by road. Our intrepid would-be volunteers were mostly making the best of things, in fact some were relishing the challenge. Others were not quite so happy and one never turned up at all.

My mind went back to the time we sat around our kitchen table, talking about how best to select volunteers to come to Zambia with us. We agreed that we would invite only people with experience and expertise or qualifications in areas, which would be of help to the projects we supported in Zambia. No unaccompanied young gap year students, for example, as we did not have the resources to support them and supervise them in Zambia. They must be positive, resilient and able to get on well with others even in challenging circumstances. This was the challenge we devised – a weekend with people they had only just met, in an isolated cottage on Dartmoor, which was hard to find and offered only the most basic accommodation. What could possibly go wrong?

Surprisingly perhaps, nothing drastic did go wrong on this weekend. It even felt quite cosy and warm at times, when we had a big fire going and were sitting around In the candlelight, telling stories and playing games.

Three of the people who had been with us on this Dartmoor weekend came with us to Zambia later and all made a very helpful and positive contribution, especially In Kantolomba, so maybe It wasn't such a crazy Idea after all.

Alan and I were lucky enough to share most of our visits to Zambia with volunteers with different skills and experience, which they generously offered. They became trusted friends as well as co-workers and we benefitted so much from their support and their company. Helen was one of our Trustees, who came to Zambia with us in later years, and supported us through good and bad times. She had worked as a senior manager with vulnerable people in Devon and had so much valuable experience to offer, when it came to planning strategy and systems and sorting out problems. We shared some good times together, but she was always one of the first to know and understand when things were not going well.

In Zambia, when you ask an ambitious child what he or she wants to do in life, the chances are that she will say she wants to be a doctor. This seems to represent the social and academic heights, so when one of our Trustees Sally, who is a GP, visited in 2007 with her husband Nick, also a GP, and their children, this was a positive experience all round. Hellen Mpundu told me that it brought status and respect to her new project Umwana Kasembe, near Lusaka, which was just struggling to get established and was meeting a lot of opposition from powerful men, at the time. Hellen admitted that she was expecting her doctor visitors to stay in a five-star hotel, rather than in a camping lodge nearby and she was impressed by their adaptability and friendliness.

Sally wrote as follows:
We were all so excited to arrive in Lusaka, weighed down with footballs/kit/netball bibs and bits of medical equipment. The plan was to deworm the children at our projects and hopefully give them a health check, to see if we could identify any soluble problems.

The projects welcomed us all and the Zambian children were delighted to chat and play with Izzy 14 and Ed 12. Meanwhile, Nick and I tried to assess the well-being of the children and volunteers. The projects we visited impressed us with their well organised food programmes. The children were getting a good meal at school, and their health, given their situation, was pretty good.

Among other illnesses the children have to contend with are worms; a de-worming programme was initiated, which involved the staff and volunteers weighing, measuring and administering the tablets to the children. This was all done in good humour and a bowl of jelly beans helped enormously! The plan was for this to be an annual event. The children were excited I think, to be weighed/measured and checked. We were impressed how healthy most of them were, including their teeth - testament to a childhood with few sweet treats.

Sadly, the few more serious conditions we identified were, we quickly realised, not going to be dealt with. Hospital treatment was not available for orphan children in Zambia at the time.

Izzy wrote
If there is one thing I will always remember it will be the kindness of people in Zambia. Everybody was so welcoming. We were met at Lusaka airport and crammed into a small car for the drive to Kantolomba. There we enjoyed various artistic and sporting performances and Ed and I tried to lend a hand on the medical side of things. The children specially made us feel so welcome, braiding my hair, teaching us games and singing. At Umwana Kasembe I probably played the most unforgettable netball match of my life, on a dusty pitch against several women with babies casually tied on their backs.

On her second visit with Liz, who is also a GP, Sally wrote:
Whilst Wendy and Alan were busy somewhere else, Liz and I were invited to join the Sisters, who were taking a hot lunch into the women's prison in Lusaka. They did this regularly. We jumped at the opportunity to see inside the prison and we were let in through a side gate and set up our servery on a small veranda. The prison was very like the compounds, dirt floors and a large

yard, with trees for shade. The women were so pleased to see us and very welcoming.

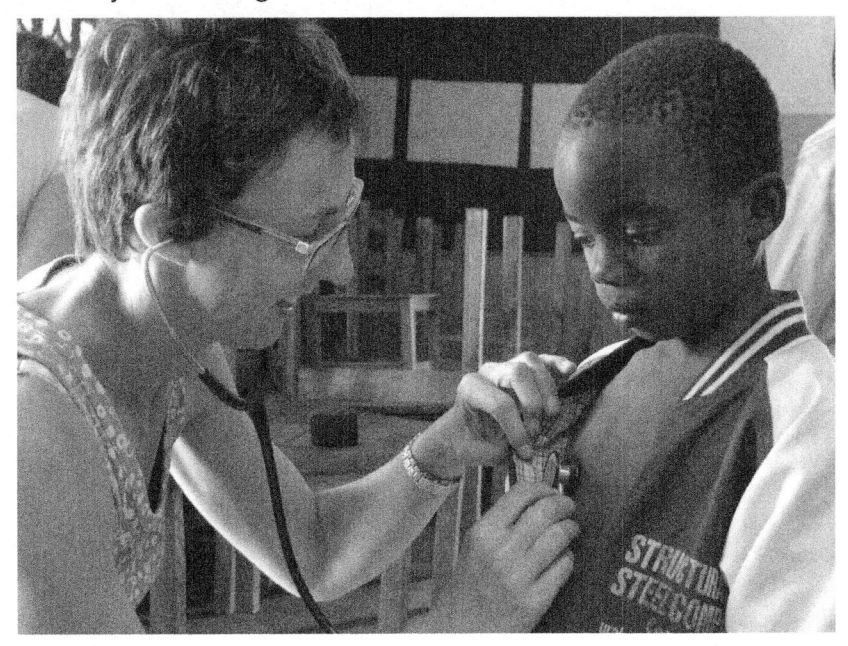

Sally in Kantolomba

There was the chance then to chat with them and play with the many small children. We had taken bags of second-hand children's clothes, which were very welcome. The women were allowed to have any children under 5 stay with them, but, after 5 they were transferred to other members of the family. It must have been very difficult for these children to leave their mothers. In some ways the prison didn't seem too bad, as many of the women already had such hard lives and poor living conditions in the compounds.

Liz wrote:
I first went to Zambia in 2008 with my daughter Joanna. We were quite nervous when we arrived and unsure what to expect. We went first to the Misisi compound in Lusaka. What struck me most was the amazingly resilient, cheerful people who are

living in the most deprived and depressing place, a place of utter deprivation. The women were the most stoical, strong people I have ever met. While there we played a hilarious netball match, as Joanna had raised money at school for the bibs and balls. I have never played a game with no rules before, but the children thoroughly enjoyed it and so did we.

My main job while there was to weigh and measure the children and to give them the appropriate doses of deworming tablets. It took a little bit of explaining to the mothers the benefits of deworming tablets as they were naturally suspicious, which was completely understandable.

We went the next day to Umwana Kasembe, which was a different set up. It was more of a drop-in centre in a township with a real problem of child abuse. There I saw children with signs I have learned to recognise as indicating child abuse. It was very difficult because there were few resources to refer the children to.

We later went further north, to visit Kantolomba and visited the very successful school which is running there. We enjoyed wonderful entertainment and singing and dancing from the children at the school. Or sometimes the women would be busy doing something, cooking the lunch or sewing, and someone would just start singing and dancing.

Considering their conditions and diet, the children's health did seem, overall, to be good, but it was difficult when you found a child who had something seriously wrong because I knew that they wouldn't be able to access X rays or hospital treatment.
I made two further trips to Zambia, one of them with Sally, who has written about our visit to the prison in Lusaka, which was not as grim as I was expecting, given the living conditions of many women in the compounds.

Despite some of the difficult experiences, there were also some very funny ones. People were always very keen to please and to say what they thought you wanted to hear and this led to some interesting situations. I remember going to a shop in Ndola which advertised copying, printing and internet access. At first the owners said that they were sorry that the photocopier was not working very well, then later admitted that it was broken. Finally they explained that they didn't actually have one! We then asked if we could use the internet and were told that it was very slow that day, but they in fact they didn't have internet access at all.

Of all my visits the overwhelming feeling is of respect, especially for Zambian women, who are the most cheerful, resilient people I have ever met.

Liz first visited Zambia with us in 2008 and some of her time was spent in Kantolomba, where she set up an informal 'clinic' mainly to administer deworming tablets. She always kicked off her shoes and was known as the 'barefoot doctor'.

Everyone who has spent time in Zambia has been touched by the enthusiasm of the children and their obvious pleasure in their lessons, their singing and dancing and sport.

Our grandson Nathan was 17 when he first came to Zambia with us and we were pleased and proud with how well he responded to everyone. He was very deeply affected by what he saw. He wrote these words, after his visit, showing some considerable insight for a 17 year old.

Impressions of Zambia, by Nathan

In Zambia the sunset is stunningly beautiful.

The fiery sun, sinking below the horizon, seems to be flying through the sky.

This spectacular switch from day to night seems to represent the lives of people in Zambia perfectly.

In the life of a poor Zambian, living in a township, nothing is permanent.

With no chance of a loan and no proof of the ownership of property, everything becomes short term.

There is little or no job opportunity and the next meal is always an uncertain event.

The baby in your arms who is clinging so tightly to your finger, is going to have to battle to survive.

Yet, as the sun sinks out of view, it paints the sky with fire.

The people's lives are filled with loss and struggle, but they overwhelm you with their warmth and energy.

All the young people who have visited Zambia with us participated fully in the activities offered, with interest and enthusiasm. They have been great ambassadors for our charity. They have themselves been influenced, by the experience in different ways and their lives have been changed by it, sometimes significantly. Nathan went on to study for a degree in International Development and now works in an international charity for people with disabilities. Nathan, Joanna, Izzy and Ed all say that the experience of visiting Zambia at this formative time of their lives had a significant influence on them.

It is worth saying, here, that these young people were family members, who were in the care of their parents or grandparents and took a lead from them. We were always careful to ensure that anyone visiting the projects in Zambia was resourceful and able to take care of themselves while in the country. It was important that we did not make extra demands on Zambian project staff and volunteers, who already had more than enough to cope with.

One of our volunteers was Neil, who went to Kantolomba with us one year. Back home in Devon, Neil and his wife Karen, were experienced and skilled foster carers. Neil was also an electrical engineer, so he had considerable skills to offer, which were put to good use in Zambia. Reminiscing with us recently, about his time there, he recalled the complete culture shock, on arriving in the country, to be met at Lusaka airport in the early morning by Musonda, Hellen's son, and taken straight into the noise and rush and pandemonium of the central bus station for the long bus journey to Ndola. An unforgettable experience for Neil: but he soon found his feet when he was introduced to a group of parents and carers in Kantolomba. The women were so impressed that he, a man, could and did look after young children, even babies and he won their respect when he walked around with a baby tied onto his back in the traditional manner!

The men were more impressed when Neil and Peter set about re-wiring the school, sourcing out of date materials from shops in Ndola and managing to complete the whole job, in boiling heat, within the week, while also demonstrating the task to others.

Ian, who was another Devon foster carer, also came with us as a volunteer, at the same time as Neil. Both enjoyed talking with families in Kantolomba who were trying to help troubled children.

But Ian had another skill to offer, which was much in demand. He was an amateur football referee. Most of the older boys were mad about football but had little idea of the rules of the game, as far as I could see. The general idea seemed to be for a pack of barefoot boys to chase around after the ball, in an area of rough ground, where passers-by frequently walked across, sometimes stopping to intercept and kick the ball, if it came their way. Ian struggled to impose a semblance of order on these games, but he did bring with him some football shirts, belonging to a Devon team. These were a great success, although they were much too large for the Zambian boys, most of whom were small and underweight. But still, it encouraged them and made them feel more like a proper team.

At Umwana Kasembe there was already a well-established football team, which was coached by local volunteers, and they played a match against the nearby prestigious private school. They usually won, despite playing barefoot and without proper kit. There was also a strong netball team for the girls and young women. Some of them played with babies still tied on their backs. Hellen always encouraged sport and other out of school activities for the children and young people in her care.

Top team Chilanga

During his work with the teachers at Kantolomba, our son Michael had tried to encourage them to expand the curriculum to include more creative and sporting activities, rather than just the 'chalk and talk' method, favoured in many Zambian schools. Michael's report is included in a previous chapter.

With this in mind, we were accompanied on one visit, by a friend Sylvia, from North Wales who was an artist. Sylvia had previously spent some time in Malawi, doing paintings of animals and wildlife and was keen to help in Zambia, when we talked to her about this. She was given generous donations of both money and art materials by her local network of painters and artists and arrived in Lusaka with a case full of beautiful art materials. The children at Umwana Kasembe were the first to benefit from this opportunity and Sylvia spent some memorable times with them, playing around with the paints and other art materials and encouraging them to try out different techniques. This was very liberating for kids who had previously been expected just to produce neat, small drawings, with pencil and paper. This was a very different experience : everyone was exhausted and covered in paint at the end of the day, but some wonderful pictures were made.

For myself, it was good to see the children and teachers being creative and enjoying themselves and the results were surprising. Some children proved to be very talented – often those you would least expect, while the quiet, studious, pupils sometimes found it too challenging to deviate from their usual style of drawing.

Another volunteer who worked with us was Sarah, who was an experienced social worker, also from Devon. Sarah had been with us on the memorable Dartmoor weekend described above and had come through with flying colours! She was always calm and resourceful in any situation and took most things in her stride. A good person to have with you in a crisis and she certainly survived a few of those. Sarah's task was to work alongside Jane, who was being sponsored by our charity to do a social work course. The two women worked well together and stayed in touch after Sarah returned to the UK.

Sarah was good at sport and swimming and later raised funds for us by doing a triathlon race, in Devon, with her partner. On one occasion we went to the public pool in Ndola with Sarah, on one of our days off. There were very few adults in the pool that day and most of the young Zambians and children were struggling to swim in the shallow end. Sarah was trying to help some children to learn to swim. I still remember the gasps of admiration when, later, she dived off the top board.

We owe a debt of gratitude to everyone who has been with us on this journey in Zambia, some for the long haul and some for a shorter time. It's not possible to speak of everyone here but I hope they know how much we appreciate what they did.

Chapter 10

Work in Lusaka

Through our work with the religious Sisters in Lusaka, we came to know a project which had been set up in one of the largest, most crowded and probably the poorest of all the compounds in central Lusaka - Misisi township. It was a grim place to visit. There was no proper drainage, sewage or rubbish collection, so the place was often flooded and outbreaks of cholera were common. There were many orphans and street children, who were dependent on begging or petty thieving, to survive. The railway line ran through the centre of the compound and was flanked on both sides by piles of rubbish. The environment was depressing, but we found that many people there were busy and active, buying and selling, carrying loads, hawking goods, touting for business from small roadside shacks.

The project we were introduced to first, consisted of a school, a skills training centre and a project for sick and dying people, as well as a temporary shelter for street children, which was in an empty shipping container. It made a good, weather proof room, but was terribly hot when the sun shone. Our charity made a financial contribution to supporting the poorest carers. They were mainly grandparents or older children, who were struggling to look after orphans and young children and to send them to school. These carers received help, such as food and clothes and school fees and sometimes micro loans, to establish small businesses. Most families were looking after 2 or 3 orphans, in addition to their own children. There was a community committee of local people, who met regularly and did their best to identify the families in the most urgent need.

We always found it difficult, when we were asked on a personal basis for help, which often happened. It was so hard to say no, but we could not give to everyone with our limited means, and the project managers always warned us against giving to individuals, as it created more problems for them.

The project manager here, Joseph, was an energetic and resourceful man, who was very active in the community, trying to get improvements to roads, garbage disposal, water and sanitation and the myriad problems which beset this compound. He always had ambitious plans for building and expansion and was a very hard worker, with an eye on every opportunity that came along. This was positive in many ways but could also be a danger, as some of these opportunities were mainly to the benefit of his own family and friends we later found out, to our cost.

The culture in Zambia means that tribal and family loyalty are more important than almost everything else. In the absence of a welfare state or income support system, families must support each other to survive. Education and health care clinics are expensive. There are many funerals to be paid for and orphans to be looked after. When so many are unemployed, the pressures from family on a relative who has a job and is doing well are immense and family demands are hard to withstand. We understood this very well, but it was hard to explain to people at home who had raised funds for us and we always felt so bad if funds were misused, which we sometimes suspected they were.

I talked to Hellen Mpundu about the problem, and she gave me her views on what may have happened. She has no proof that things have gone astray but she has suspicions. Again, it is hard to see where the truth may lie. Yet somehow there is still joy and laughter and generosity and a new day tomorrow.

From my diary
On Sunday we went to church with the Sisters. Alan and I crowded onto the benches at the back, amongst the women

and babies, little cute fat babies all around us, sweating under layers of woolly hats, jumpers, socks and blankets. Beautiful singing, the waves of sound rising and falling, as the choir leaders stood at the front, bringing in their sections, to swell the harmonies, first the women's voices, then the deep bass of the men. Heads turned, to see the procession gathering outside, for this was a special celebration of some kind. First the clergy and their attendants and hangers on, all in white robes. They were followed by a group of young girls, dressed alike in clothes of shiny material, with veils on their heads and plastic flowers in their hair: they danced in formation up the aisle, with intricate footwork and arms waving above their heads. After that came the women in their sections, their matronly figures clothed in traditional wraps. They danced in a more stately manner, shuffling their feet and swaying to the music. Finally came the gifts for the clergy, chickens, bags of maize, a young woman danced forward, with an enormous basket of fruit on her head. Children brought packets of sugar, salt or a few vegetables. No matter how poor, they give generously to the clergy. It is plain to see that this is the highlight of the week for many people. The choirs from different sections of the township practise regularly for these occasions and they sing with a joy and passion which moves me to tears.

Afterwards we walked through the township with a Zambian friend and had lunch in her little house, while she chatted about her life, the price of things, school fees, her son's chance of getting a place at college. It was refreshing to spend time with her and her family. She does so well with what she has and has managed to build another room onto her house this year, paying for roofing sheets and a few bricks at a time from her wages. Her son is a tall, good looking young man and, later, he walked us back through the narrow lanes of the township to the main road.

Other work in Misisi township

The AIDS pandemic had affected thousands of families in Lusaka and all over Zambia. Many of those we met had suffered bereavement and were looking after orphan children or they were very sick themselves. Many children who had lost parents ended up living with other relatives and sometimes in another part of the country, where nobody knew the important things about their background. We saw that children were often very confused and disturbed by a lack of understanding of the past and that surviving relatives were struggling to cope. Amanda and I were asked to organise some kind of a training workshop in Misisi to attempt to help with this.

We had brought with us a selection of puppets, to help us to tell a story about bereavement and loss in a way which children and their carers might understand. We called this 'Humphrey's Journey' and it was based on a method used in the UK by a remarkable woman called Dr Sheila Cassidy, who used a toy bear and his animal friends to illustrate her story, 'Jeremiah's Journey'. Amanda had worked with Dr Cassidy and had adapted her idea for our children and families in Zambia.

Bears being a rarity in Zambia, we decided to make our toy animal a Hippo, Humphrey, and to give him a selection of African animal friends. Our families back home helped us to get together some small toys for this purpose, most of them hand knitted originals. On one occasion we were maybe not as sensitive as we might have been to local cultural issues, because, when we produced a snake, in our story, the women in the group screamed and ran for the door!

As well as this work on bereavement, we also organised a workshop to help relatives to pass on precious family memories to their children and grandchildren. This involved making 'memory boxes', and we found that it was effective and popular with the women, especially since some of them were themselves HIV positive.

From my diary

On the day of the workshop, Amanda and I collected up all the boxes, paper, scissors, shiny stars, ribbons, glitter, glue, puppets and other things and loaded them into the van. These are for the women to make their memory boxes, to put in the keepsakes, things which are important in their own lives and family history, which they wanted to pass on to their children. Photos are a rarity in most families, so the memory boxes might contain pieces of material, beads, a plait of hair, dried plants, stones, knitted or embroidered cloths, each with a special significance and memory attached. As we drove into the compound, we saw that some of the women had already arrived and we heard them talking together. Some were busy getting things ready for the lunch outside and we could see a basket of desperate looking chickens, gasping for breath. I tried not to dwell on the fact that we would be eating them in a few hours' time; at least they would be fresh!

As the workshop got under way, the women shared painful memories, and some became very emotional, but there was laughter as well as tears and we were amazed at how incredibly brave and resourceful most of the women were. When it was time to construct their memory boxes, there was a scramble for the best materials, with some people trying to monopolise the scissors and glue and stars. But as they got into making the boxes and putting in their keepsakes, a silence fell on the group, with everyone absorbed in their task. Soon, one of the women started to sing, very softly, and the song was taken up, in harmony, by the others as the sound rose and fell in the room, like a wave. I felt the tears pricking my eyes and I could see Amanda was struggling not to cry, as we thought of what these women have already lost. But there was love and compassion flowing through the music, straight to our hearts.

There was a lot of good work going on in this township, most of it involving the women. When we visited, early in 2005, we were accompanied by Carolyn, a young journalist, the daughter of Helen, one of our Trustees. She was very impressed by the tailoring school, where a group of young women were busy putting the finishing touches to the garments they had been working on all year. The sewing machines were going ninety to the dozen, as they worked on the outfits for their graduation, which was the following week. There were beautiful, intricate traditional outfits in green and gold, as well as business outfits, sports kit and several sets of baby clothes and knitted shawls.

Amanda, Carolyn and I were invited to attend this graduation, which was held in the new community hall, built with donations from a parish in Ireland.

From my diary
I drove into Misisi this morning, with Ester, the young woman we are sponsoring to study for a degree in education at the University of Zambia. Ester knows her way around of course, having grown up here. Amanda and Carolyn and I sat outside the school, where Ester was teaching us some Bemba songs – a lovely start to the day. After some time we filed into the new hall for the graduation of the tailoring students. There followed a very long wait and there were speeches and false starts, while music played and people wandered in and out at random. We sat around for ages waiting for the party to begin. Joseph sat us like VIPs up on the platform, to our embarrassment, then disappeared to organise something. At last the students came dancing in, resplendent in their new outfits and applauded by their friends and relatives.

At a crucial moment during the presentation of certificates a large fridge for drinks was ceremoniously carried in by two brawny young men and set in a place of honour on the stage. Then more speeches. I wished the ground would swallow me up when the headmaster, a pompous, garrulous man, introduced me as 'the Queen Mother of Zambia' to loud laughter from my compatriots! After another long wait, eventually the food arrived, cold and overcooked, but there were not enough customers to eat it as most people had given up and drifted away by this time. Fortunately, nothing was wasted, as the children who had been shut out, but were looking in through the holes in the wall, found their way inside and polished off the leftovers. Then the dancing broke out and the party really began. We all joined in with the dancing and I was happy to see Ester relaxed, dancing and enjoying herself.

Alan and I were quite frequently in Misisi during our visits to Zambia and we could not help but be impressed by the ways in which some of the inhabitants worked to improve their lives, despite their depressing surroundings. An enterprising group of women came to see me with a good idea: they wanted to produce their own sunflower oil. They knew very well that food was the one thing they could be sure to sell in the compound, even if people had no money for anything else. One of the staples of the Zambian diet is sunflower oil, which is used to cook the vegetables, tomatoes, onions, local kale or rape leaves, which go to make a relish, or stew, sometimes with ground nuts added. This is always served with a portion of Nshima (maize meal porridge). Meat, fish, or chicken is often unaffordable for the poorest people. Fried foods are popular and we often passed stalls selling fritters, which could consist of various things coated in batter, fried in oil and seasoned.

The women wanted to produce a homemade version, which could be both cheaper and purer than the oil sold in shops. There was a company in Zambia which had developed small, hand operated presses for extracting the oil from sunflower seeds. I think it was operating in Tanzania as well. There was a branch in Lusaka which gave demonstrations of the oil press in action and I took a group of women to learn how to operate it. This involved filling a hopper with sunflower seed and pulling down a very heavy lever each time the hopper was filled. I doubted if some of the older women would manage it, although most of them were much stronger than me and used to hard physical work. We arranged to buy a press anyway, with a donation from our village at home, and the project soon got underway. The older women played their part by helping with the straining, bottling, labelling and selling of the oil when it was ready.

The sunflower seeds had to be warmed, before being pressed and this was achieved by spreading out the seeds on black plastic in the sunshine for a while. No need to warm them artificially; sunshine was pretty well guaranteed from March to November in this part of Zambia. There were some problems in sourcing cheap sunflower seed, of course, but anyway, it produced excellent oil, with no artificial additives, an improvement on the varieties currently available.

Meanwhile, Alan got to know a group of older, unemployed men in Misisi, who called themselves the Bakalamba. It can be approximately translated, ironically, as 'the old boys'. They also formed themselves into a group and their proposal was to make bricks, since there was always a demand for new building in Lusaka. For this they needed some basics such as sand, cement, spades, shovels, and a wheelbarrow. We managed to get hold of these things, and the men named themselves company directors, chairman, vice chairman, secretary and treasurer and so on. Whatever they were called, they worked very hard, and produced good quality bricks for sale. They got a large order, with payment in advance, from one of the Sisters and this enabled them to buy materials and get well established at an early stage. They were very successful and even began to give lessons to other groups in entrepreneurship.

Misisi Township in 2006

Chapter 11

A significant year

When I look back over the years and many visits to Zambia, the year 2008 always comes to my mind. It encapsulates many of the contradictions, the joy and the sadness, the things that worked out and some that failed. In 2007 I had a serious illness, which kept me at home for some months. Other members of our team visited Zambia during that year, in our place, but in the spring of 2008, Alan and I were keen to get back again and see for ourselves how things were getting on. We set off in April, full of enthusiasm and with the added pleasure of taking with us our Grandson, Nathan, who was then 17 and a friend, Liz, who is a GP and her daughter, Joanna, a similar age to Nathan. It was a positive learning experience for the young people and we were very proud of them and of how they behaved. Liz got on well with everyone, took it all in her stride, worked hard and visited Zambia several times with us subsequently.

My Diary
I am sitting up in bed under a large mosquito net, writing this by the light of a head torch. Cicadas are chirping outside, tree frogs are croaking and there are bright stars overhead. We are in Eureka camp site, which has lots of beautiful mopane trees. Alan is asleep beside me and Nathan sitting outside on the veranda. This campsite is quiet, away from the road, with sounds of the bush all around. We have seen monkeys, zebra and impala and some giraffe. Nathan met buffalo and ostriches when he was out for a run this morning. I envy Alan, who can sleep soundly anywhere, but for me it is the start of another long night.

At the weekend, we were invited to visit the Sisters, on the other side of Lusaka. We had a lovely evening with them, and I was so happy to see them again after being away from Zambia last year.

I was pleased and proud to introduce them to Nathan, Liz and Joanna. We had a convivial evening, with lots of chat about old times, but soon enough it was time for us to leave and to head back to our campsite. One of the Sisters called a taxi for us: she knew a local man who needed the money and charged a reasonable price. We had a memorable journey!

There was a hooting at the gate and we said a fond goodbye to our friends before going out into the warm night. There were five of us, a slightly problematic number for a taxi which is only supposed to take four passengers. However, the taxi man didn't mind about this, as we climbed into his battered vehicle. Lusaka is not a good place to be on a dark night. There are no streetlights, and the roads are full of potholes, which necessitate a kind of slalom action, when driving, to avoid the deepest of them.

The lights on our taxi were very dim and it was not in good shape, but the driver assured us that he is a very good mechanic and had fixed up the vehicle himself. He told us a lot more about himself than we really wanted to hear and kept up a stream of talk until we reached the other side of the city. At this point the car started to cough and splutter. By now we were on the main road south, which leads eventually to Livingstone: heavy lorries roar along here on their way to Kafue and it is bordered for much of the way by bush. Here the taxi came to a complete stop. "No problem, madam," the driver assured us. "I will have it fixed in a minute." We soon realised that we had well and truly broken down, probably due to not having any petrol in the tank. The chances of this vehicle moving any time soon began to look small.

"How far are we from the camp?" Liz asked.

"I guess about half an hour walk from the entrance to the park," Alan said, "but it's not very safe for walking, maybe we'd be better staying put."

"Oh come on, said Liz, we could be here for hours. There are five of us, what could happen to us? Let's walk!"

We paid off the driver, still insisting that his friend was coming soon, and set off down the pathway at the side of the road. The night was dark and full of rustlings.

"What about snakes?" Joanna asked, nervously.

"Oh, don't worry, if we just stamp our feet and make a noise they will keep well away," Alan said, with false confidence. We stepped out stoutly, singing and talking as we went, but it did seem a very long way. Occasionally a heavy truck roared past, its lights sweeping across the road and illuminating the bush around us. When it passed, the darkness felt even deeper. At last we reached the drive to the camping park, but our problems were not yet over: the entrance was guarded by a very large dog. Alan had supposedly made friends with this dog but it didn't seem to recognise him.

"Just call it, let it know you are a friend," we suggested.

"I can't remember its damned name," Alan tried a few names, as the dog prowled around us and, "here boy, good dog."

Eventually the dog approached Alan in what seemed a friendly way, while the rest of us shrank back and left him to it.

We hurried on, down the long drive back to our cabins and were very glad to get safely to our beds that night.

We were back to work the next day and were planning to visit Hellen's project, Umwana Kasembe, which was quite close to the camping park. During the daytime, buses passed regularly along the main road, so we were able to reach it easily.

Hellen came to the campsite in the morning and we spent a long time talking budgets and trying to put together a funding bid. Neither of us are expert at this and we found it hard to get our heads around it. It's so difficult to predict what may be needed two years from now and how things will develop. Hellen's great strength is to make the most of opportunities as they arise, to innovate, improvise and make do with what she has. This needs flexible funding which we, as a small organisation, can provide but larger ones apparently cannot. Hellen and I really struggled with the figures.

I went with Alan into Misisi township in Lusaka later. We visited some pharmacies to get worming tablets and paracetamol for Liz to administer. Misisi looked awful, with stagnant pools everywhere and foul-smelling water. Alan and I returned to the campsite in mid-afternoon, very unsettled by what we saw in Misisi. We paid a visit to the community project we supported which was managed by Joseph but found that it was deserted and looked neglected. They were not expecting a visit from us, of course, but nevertheless, it was strange that there was nobody around.

The next day we all took the bus into Lusaka and met Joseph at his school. We saw a completely different picture today. All the teachers, children and parents had gathered for a prizegiving day. We were asked to give out clothes and books to the children in each class who had the best results. It was lovely to see the proud parents and carers, hugging their children, who had done so well. Joseph surprised us by giving us presents too and made a moving speech when we protested "There is no hand so poor that it cannot give and no hand so rich that it cannot receive", he said. All very touching and emotional.

We returned to Chilanga on the bus and went to Umwana Kasembe, where Hellen and her women helpers had prepared some wonderful traditional food for us, with okra, sweet potato leaves, pumpkin leaves, nuts and berries, tomatoes and onions. All grown in their own land and little gardens. It's so rare to be served food like this in the places we usually eat in Zambia. The cafes in town serve things like chicken and chips, steak and chips and pasties. We shared the food Hellen gave us with the volunteers and children and had a sociable time together.

A visit to Kantolomba.

The next day we went up to Ndola by minibus, leaving early in the morning. What luxury, after so many terrible bus journeys! Joseph had business in the Copperbelt and had offered to take us. We booked into a guest house and settled in. Henry, the manager at Kantolomba, came to meet with us in the evening to sort out our program for the week.

In the morning we went into Kantolomba in a local taxi. The road is still very rough, and we had to get out, as the driver eased the car over a gully full of stones. We got a great welcome and Henry took us over to the skills centre, where a spectacular performance had been prepared for us; singing and drama and dancing. Our visitors were quite overwhelmed by it all. It was lovely to see the children enjoying themselves and playing under the avocado tree in the shade.

The Centre is finished and looks good, but very little is happening there: no carpentry, tailoring, kiosk or chickens — none of the things that were planned. Apparently, the electricity has not yet been connected at the skills centre and that was the given reason for the lack of progress, but I felt uneasy. Was something going wrong? Alan and I were planning to talk to the teachers tomorrow, so maybe that would enlighten us. Meanwhile Nathan and Joanna walked around the township with two older boys, while Liz got started talking to the children, weighing and measuring them.

We managed to get deworming tablets in town later, after much hassle, going to different pharmacies to get the requisite number of tablets, but eventually we were successful.

The next day there should have been sports at the field, but it was abandoned because there were too many funerals this morning and the field is right next to the burial ground. It was a stark reminder of the terrible number of deaths locally and the fact that the school is in a desperately poor area. Alan went off into the community with the social worker, talking to carers, while Liz was examining children and administering worming tablets. Nathan was helping her. I spent much of the morning with Perry, the senior teacher, who is well qualified and has a lovely way with the children. Later, we took the teachers to a cafe in town for a meal, and I spoke to them one by one about their work and their concerns. Everyone spoke cautiously, I felt. They need more resources of course but there didn't seem to be too many other concerns, fortunately, or none that were voiced.

The next morning, we were with Henry and the new social worker, talking over ideas and agreeing objectives for the future, but it was slow going. They were agreeing with what we suggested but there seemed to be little enthusiasm or detailed information about their work. Later we met with Mr P the independent accountant, who also voiced some concerns about the management of the project. We discussed it all when we returned to the guest house and I had another sleepless night.

This visit to Kantolomba was significant, as we look back on subsequent events. The skills centre, which we raised funds for and Peter designed, had been completed to a good standard and we were keen to see what developments there had been. Although the visit was enjoyable and positive in many ways, afterwards Alan and I were left with an uneasy feeling. But we were unsure what to do. There was so little time, and we were not there to manage the project ourselves: our role was to agree aims and objectives with the staff, to observe, to listen, to encourage and suggest, and to check that all was going well. We could not pin it down but we felt that something was wrong. We were also very conscious of our responsibility to our donors to try to ensure that the aims of the charity were carried out. We were soon to find out that our premonitions were all too true.

A few months later, after we returned home, we had a phone call from one of the teachers, giving us information about the management of Kantolomba school. It was obvious that things had gone very wrong and the manager had been misusing funds. We had to act quickly. We got together with our Trustees and, after a very emotional and upsetting meeting, it was decided that an emergency visit was needed.

Alan went immediately to Zambia. I was unable to go at that time, but we talked every night on the phone: we had some difficult decisions to make. He found our worst fears confirmed, when he arrived at the school in Kantolomba. It was virtually deserted, with no children around. Members of the community came forward, when they saw Alan, to tell him about the situation and he sought out some of the teachers, who told him more. He went to look for the manager, at his home and found him very defensive, at first, but the evidence was clear to see. After a very difficult meeting, Henry finally admitted his dishonesty.

As a team, we decided there was no alternative but to close things down temporarily until we could make a fresh start with a new manager. Fortunately, this did not take long, as the head teacher at the school was willing to take on the task temporarily, on a trial basis. Once a new bank account was set up, with the help of our accountant in Zambia, we began to send funds again and the school was soon back in business.

This was a very difficult time for us all and we are sad that the children and families at Kantolomba missed out on their education for a while, due to the dishonesty of the manager. We did the best we could to rescue the situation as soon as possible. This was especially hard for Alan, who was on the spot, and found it very upsetting. But, as so often in Zambia, even amid the worst crises he was able to find moments of humour.

Here is his description of an evening towards the end of his visit: It had been a hell of a day and I returned to the guest house feeling beat up. Hoping for a quiet beer, I went into the lobby, where there were a few easy chairs and a television. The bar was closed, but I found all the staff gathered around the TV, looking solemn. I enquired what had happened and was told that it was a ceremony for the late President, who had died only a few days previously. He was a popular man. I expressed my regrets at his passing, of course, and sat down to watch with them. Sad and solemn music was played, and various dignitaries came to the platform to make speeches in honour of the late president. One by one they came up, in their robes and uniforms, with much gold braid and medals on display. The army was in attendance and a twenty-one-gun salute was called for by the head of the armed forces. The camera panned to the soldiers who were kneeling by their guns. There was silence and another call was made for a gun salute, as the camera revealed the kneeling soldiers. Again, no action. Finally, the head of the Judiciary came forward, in his white wig and robes and began his speech. At that point the guns suddenly got going and his voice was drowned out by deafening explosions, as clouds of smoke drifted across the stage, obscuring everyone on the platform and some of the mourners as well. I very much regret to say that I burst out laughing. After the stress of the day, the release of tension was too much, and I saw the funny side. Understandably, others certainly didn't, and I had to apologise and make a hasty retreat.

Despite the occasional humour, this experience was really hard for Alan, but he found support and understanding from the Sisters, who warmly welcomed him, when he returned to Lusaka the following day. They also had experienced difficulties and disappointments during their many years in Zambia and knew only too well how he would be feeling.

The community school at Kantolomba was reorganised after this, and soon acquired a new name 'Ulupwa' which means, in Bemba 'The whole family' an approximate translation of 'Families for Children'. The new manager was the former headteacher, Perry and he made a good start, eager to prove himself and keen to learn new skills. He was a quiet man, very gentle with the children and an excellent teacher. He was amenable and easy to work with and he spoke good English.

A few months later, we returned to see how things were progressing. We were pleased to see that all seemed to be going well. Perry and his new social worker, Patience, had a lot of problems to sort out initially but, by the end of the year they seemed to have gained the trust of the local community and there were more that 350 children attending the school daily. There was a new management committee of local people, who were involved in the decision making and planning for the project.

We were still the main donors but Outi and family in Finland were also faithfully supporting Kantolomba and, once we had reported back to Outi that all seemed to be well, they renewed their regular funding for the school.

Over the next three years our visits to Kantolomba were reassuring and it was always a great pleasure to meet with the children, teachers and volunteers and to see how much they enjoyed their school. Educationally they were thriving, and the senior children were successfully progressing to one of the governments run high schools. For this they needed sponsorship because these schools were not free, and the Ulupwa project was able to sponsor several children, from their budget.

But there was little progress towards income generation, despite our funding some capital projects. One of the capital projects was the procuring of a hammer mill to grind maize, for the staple food in Zambia. Some time later we were fortunate to receive a generous donation from a donor in London, to buy the hammer mill, which had to be purchased from a supplier in Lusaka. In theory, the hammer mill should have provided the Kantolomba community with an income but it seemed to take forever to get it up and running and it was never a money spinner.

We made several other attempts to fund small income generation projects, such as one to repair bicycles. One of these was very memorable: we met a group of local boys in Kantolomba, who seemed dead keen to set themselves up as bicycle repair men. They purchased T shirts and repair kits, with funds we donated, and arranged a meeting with us. They gave themselves titles such as chairman, deputy, secretary and treasurer and we were touched by their enthusiasm. Unfortunately, after a few months, they had to report back to us that they had no customers. Apparently, nobody owned a bicycle in this very poor community, or those that did must have repaired their own!

We often look back on this time, as being difficult and disappointing in many ways, yet there were many humorous incidents too and we never quite knew what might happen next.

Chapter 12

Sponsored students

Ester

After our difficult experiences at Kantolomba, it is good to turn to something more positive. One of the things that makes me happy is hearing about the students we sponsored into further education. The first of these was Ester, who graduated with a first class degree in education from the University of Zambia. I met her again recently and it was a great pleasure to spend time with her and to learn how well she is getting on.

We first met Ester, while doing some work in Misisi Township, in central Lusaka. She was a sweet faced, serious looking girl, who seemed nervous and was very respectful to us. We were told that Ester had come from a caring family, with a father who was employed, but both her parents had died, leaving her without any means of support. She was currently living with her older brother and his family: her mother had died quite recently. Ester had managed to complete her secondary education, and had done well in her grade 12 exams, with hard work and determination and some sporadic sponsorship from family friends or relatives. At one point a local priest paid her school fees for a while.

Everyone recognised that Ester was a hard worker and very serious in her ambition to go to university. Like many other talented and able young people, her goal was to be a medical doctor, despite the very remote chance of this becoming a reality. We talked to her about her ambitions and were impressed with her single minded and serious approach. We decided to put to our Trustees the possibility of sponsoring her to go on to university. This was a long-term commitment, but we felt that she deserved the chance.

Shortly afterwards, Ester began the process of applying to the University of Zambia Medical school, but places seemed to be reserved only for members of what Ester called 'the upper class'. Her academic qualifications were excellent, but she had no family connections in medical or other professions, and this proved an insurmountable barrier. This was such a disappointment, but in true Ester fashion, she didn't let it daunt her spirit, but went ahead with an application to complete a degree in Education at the university of Zambia instead. She was accepted and completed her course with distinction. Four years later, she graduated from the school of education with the best results for a female student in her year.

We have seen Ester regularly over the years and have kept in touch with her progress, as she became a secondary school teacher and later completed a master's degree. When I met with her recently, I was so happy to see that she has done well and is happy with her life. She is a respected senior teacher, earning a good salary and she owns her own home, but she still keeps in regular contact with her relatives in Lusaka and does not forget her roots. We shared some memories about the past and she told me more about her upbringing and education and the obstacles she faced.

These are her words:
My life in Misisi was full of challenges. It was a community where a girl child was seen as a source of income. Most parents preferred to educate a boy child, as they believed he would take care of them when they get old. Parents would rather marry off their girl child early or even underage and benefit from the bride price the groom would pay. A few of my friends were married off in Grade 7. My case was different, as my parents believed in educating their children, regardless of their sex.

At home we usually had extended family members visiting. We

would be more than ten people in our house; some would sleep in the living room and some in the kitchen.

My school experience was not good as I was stigmatised by the other kids because of where I lived. So many negative things were associated with Misisi compound. So I started saying that I was from a nearby township and they believed me, because I used to go to school looking very clean, unlike most kids from Misisi. My parents were good people, though not educated. They got married in their local village and moved to Lusaka to look for a job. My father was a driver and worked for different organisations.

We were among the few families that lived comfortably, as dad was able to provide for us. Things became very bad when he died, as all the children were still young. My older brother dropped out of school and started a business and my older sister also dropped out and became pregnant. But I vowed to take myself out of Misisi

I am the only one in our large family who managed to complete Grade 12 and, with your help, go to university.

Ester makes light of the challenges she faced but the compound where she grew up was one of the worst for pollution, poverty, disease, drunkenness and lawlessness. There were so many orphan children who had become street kids and had turned to prostitution or thieving, to survive. Ester was an inspiration for her wider family and for other girls in her community.

Whenever we met her, on our regular visits to Zambia, Ester looked happy and well dressed, smiling and pleased to see us; it was always a joy to spend time with her. On one occasion, when she came to see us, she invited us to come and visit her room at UNZA (the university of Zambia) The university is sited in a large area of parkland, with a lake and trees where students can stroll and find a peaceful place to sit and read. But the buildings themselves were shabby and run down and lacking in some basic facilities at this time. Ester shared a tiny room and a single bed with another girl, who she had known for ten years and was at school with. Their room was immaculate and very tidy and she seemed happy with it, although she had very few clothes or other possessions. We gave her extra money for clothes and bits and pieces she needed but Ester never asked us for anything extra and was so appreciative that we were able to sponsor her degree. She managed very well on what she had. Ester graduated with flying colours, the best in her year. This was even more remarkable, given her background and the barriers she had to overcome to get there.

Ester. A teacher now

Mark

Mark is the youngest son of Anna, who worked for the Sisters in Lusaka. Anna, who speaks excellent English, became a good friend to me and told me something of her early life. She had a very difficult childhood and many problems to overcome, but brought up her three children, as a single parent, after her husband left. Anna is a very honest and intelligent woman, as well as a reliable worker and was determined to make a better life for her own children. She did a fantastic job.

Mark was still in primary school when we first met him but it was evident from quite a young age that he was clever and ambitious: With the help of some good friends from UK, we were able to support him through school and he graduated with top marks at Grade 12. Subsequently he went on to train as a chartered accountant. This was quite an achievement for a young man who was brought up in a very poor township, but he was determined and worked hard. He graduated a few years ago, got married last year and is now playing his part to support his mother and family. His hard-working mother has recently been able to retire, with the support of her children and she now has time to rest and enjoy her grandchildren.

Mark

Crispin

Crispin was living in one of the poorest townships in Lusaka when we met him and he was the head of his family, although still young himself. Both his parents had passed away and he had several younger brothers and sisters. He was so good with young children and a very kind and compassionate young man. He really wanted to become a nurse and was accepted for training in Lusaka. He continued for two years, but had many setbacks and financial problems, despite the funding we sent for his studies. In the end he found that the need to support his family and pay for the education of his younger siblings was just too strong and he was unable to cope with the competing demands on his time and his finances. His first loyalty had to be to his family and he gave up his studies. This was sad for him and disappointing for us, but so very understandable and we could not fault him for putting his family's needs first.

Jane

Jane was already a mature young woman when we first met her and was working as an administrator in a small primary school in Lusaka. We were sponsoring some of the poorest and most vulnerable children to attend this school at the time. She impressed us very much with her dedication to her work, her care and love for the children and her honesty in coming forward to disclose some bad practice and cheating in the school. She lost her job as a result. Jane was looking for a way to train as a social worker and we could see that she would be a good one. We decided to sponsor her training, and this worked out very well for Jane and for ourselves. She proved to be hard working, honest and reliable, good at keeping in touch and very helpful and loyal to us, both before and after she graduated. She has had an interesting and successful career as a social worker since then.

It was so satisfying to be able to help young people to get themselves educated and launched into a satisfying career and we were lucky with the people we sponsored. They were mostly able to take full advantage of the opportunities offered, although not always in the ways we had anticipated. For example, Ester was not able to enrol in medical training, even though we had obtained sponsorship for her from a local GP practice, here in Devon. The barriers to entry for someone from her background, in Zambia at the time, were just too high and inflexible. She tells me that things have improved now, in that respect and that is good to hear. But anyway, she did brilliantly with her alternative course and is a shining example to others.

Crispin's hopes to become a nurse were not realised, but there were many other problems he had to deal with and our Trustees were sympathetic to that.

We knew the background of poverty and deprivation that these students came from and it was a great pleasure for us to be able to support them to lift themselves out of this and to attain a better quality of life.

It was, of course, very expensive to sponsor students in this way and we could only do it for a small number, unfortunately. We were able to reach a much larger number of children by supporting their primary education, both through school and by promoting good parenting through working with families.

Township scene

Chapter 13

Fundraising

Hellen Mpundu was always coming up with different ways to raise funds and sometimes she received random, generous gifts from people who had heard about her work with children. They were not always people you would expect to be interested in this kind of work, but we were happy to accept help from anyone, within reason. On one occasion a very wealthy man in Lusaka became interested in the project and was impressed by the plight of the children. He invited me and Sally and Liz, who were in Lusaka with us at the time, for cocktails at his luxurious mansion. We had been playing with the children at Umwana Kasembe earlier and were wearing our usual well-worn jeans and T shirts, feeling a bit out of place. It felt very strange to be sitting by a film star pool in a beautiful garden, after spending the morning in the township. Our host offered a generous donation for the children but there were conditions attached. The money was to be in cash and must be spent within the week, with receipts provided. Hellen had already met this man and was unsure about whether he would deliver. She gave us a list of things urgently needed for the children, for his approval, and we talked to him about this, as we sat in the shade on the veranda. To be fair, he readily agreed on an amount of money, which we could collect from the bank on a certain day. This all had to be completed in a rush, for reasons I never really understood and didn't question too closely.

From my diary
I woke up early this morning, feeling nervous about the day. I had arranged to meet Hellen at the bank in Cairo Road, in the centre of Lusaka, to collect some money promised by the donor we met last week. As I drove to the bank, I had serious doubts about it all but, sure enough, Hellen was there to meet me, as arranged, with a large wad of bank notes in her hand. The Cairo

Road is not a good place to hang around with rolls of cash, so she jumped in the van and we headed off straight away to the Manda Hill shopping mall, with a list of items we had to get today. Most of the children needed shoes, so the first stop was a shoe shop, where we had to buy 50 pairs of shoes in different sizes. The shop assistant was overwhelmed and called the manager to help. I doubt if they ever had such a large order before and they both ran around distracted, trying to find suitable shoes. But the shoes seemed to be in random sizes, and soon the floor of the shop was covered in shoe boxes and odd shoes, while we crawled around trying to find matching pairs. Eventually we managed to find enough shoes, all in very different styles, but our shopping day was not going as planned. The next stop was a large warehouse where second hand clothes are sold. The place is cavernous and piled to the roof with bales of clothes, toys, and various other second-hand items. It was all overseen by a handsome Lebanese man, with brilliant blue eyes and I talked to him while we did our shopping. Hellen warned me that the ragged clothes are sometimes put in the centre of the bales, with the good ones on the outside. She was amused when I asked the man to open the bales for us to see, but we picked our way through the best of the clothes and toys to find what we wanted.

Second hand clothes, known as Salaula, were big business in Zambia at this time. Salaula is from a Bemba word, which means "To rummage through a pile". There was certainly plenty of rummaging going on when Carolyn, a journalist friend, went there with Ester, one of our sponsored students. Ester was expert at sorting the good from the poor quality and picking out bargains.

Carolyn later wrote an article about this for a London paper. Some of the clothes had labels from shops such as M&S, Topshop, and even Burberry and more expensive makes, as well as football shirts from premier league teams, which were much sought after. The second-hand clothing trade provides many people with the means of earning a modest income. It is also an essential source of clothing for poorer Zambians, who are just as proud of their appearance as any of us. In fact, when we visited projects like Umwana Kasembe or Kantolomba or attended functions, often we were conscious that we looked very dowdy and untidy, in comparison with most of the Zambian people there. They were invariably immaculate, with clean, ironed clothes and great style. The women usually protected their clothes while working, by covering their skirts with 'Chitenge'; these are lengths of traditional, colourful, African prints, which have a multitude of uses. They can be a skirt, a dress, an apron, a sling to carry a baby, an umbrella, a tablecloth or a floor covering. The material can also be made into colourful shirts, dresses or suits for both men and women. Hellen favoured this style of dress and usually wore traditional outfits and head wraps, which she had made herself in colourful prints. She looked marvellous in them.

I hope we managed to pick out some good quality Salaula and new shoes for the children at Umwana Kasembe that day, but unfortunately, we were not there to see when it was all given out, later in the week.

Water
One of the most intractable problems was to ensure a reliable water supply at Umwana Kasembe. We were able to raise the funds for a pump and a tank to store water, but the supply from the local council was erratic and Hellen discovered that the pipe had been cut. She managed to get it reconnected but what was really needed was a borehole, to maintain a reliable water supply. This meant more funding. But we were fortunate to receive a grant from a Rotary club in the UK for this. There was great excitement at Umwana Kasembe, when the drill arrived and, after a long time, it finally struck water.

For me, raising funds was sometimes a difficult area. I felt so uncomfortable asking people for money, even though most of the people we asked seemed more than happy to contribute. I didn't want to emphasise the plight of the people we were trying to help in Zambia too much, for fear of representing them as powerless or objects of pity. This was one issue. The other was the fear of encouraging a culture of dependence or even dishonesty in our Zambian partners. We had seen this happen so often with other organisations and certainly at government level. To try to safeguard against this, we sent out just small amounts of money on a regular basis, to enable the projects we supported to work, day to day, in their communities. We understood that an ostentatious display of resources might attract jealousy, envy or be a temptation to cheat and it was better to keep a low profile. We sent everything we raised to our Zambian projects, as we had no paid staff in the UK, but we never sent too much money at once.

There was one exception to this, when we decided to support the request for a hammer mill, to grind the maize which the project was growing in Kantoloma, as previously mentioned. It was hoped that this would provide the project with an income, for the future, as there were no other hammer mills in the area at the time.

Around this time, as luck would have it, there was a chance meeting between one of our supporters and the director of a company dealing with venture capital, in London. As a result of this meeting, Alan and I were invited to go to the offices of the company at a city centre address in London on a day designated for charity giving. On this day, a percentage of profits generated by deals on the stock market are sometimes given to selected charities

We had no idea what to expect on the day, but we volunteered to go and meet the company directors and employees, to tell them more about our charity 'Families for Children Zambia'.

The morning we spent there was unforgettable:

My Diary
We arrived in London, wearing our best clothes, me in a skirt and jacket and Alan in a suit and tie. It was freezing cold and we made our way to the company's office, which is at a very prestigious address. We took a lift to the reception, where we were greeted by a man dressed as a lion, who welcomed us warmly and introduced us to a colleague dressed as the tin man and a woman dressed as Dorothy. There was also a scarecrow and other characters from the Wizard of Oz. We felt distinctly under dressed. The drink was flowing, and we were offered a choice: Alan had a Guinness and I had a gin and tonic, although I would really have preferred a coffee at this hour. However, everyone else seemed to be drinking, so we joined in.

The Lion and the Tin man and the others carried on sitting at their computers, watching columns of figures, talking rapidly on their phones. All seemed to be going well, because by lunchtime we understood that our charity was to be the recipient of a generous donation. We didn't yet know how much but were anxious to hear. We were advised that the position should be clearer by the end of the day, so had to contain our impatience. At this point everyone headed off to a nearby pub, where many drinks were set up on the bar. On the way, we mingled with other groups of stockbrokers and office workers, attired as characters from legend or fairy tales. We had a drink with Robin Hood and Maid Marion, who were still sober enough to make conversation with us. In fact, everyone seemed lucid, except Alan and me. At last we heard the good news that our charity was to receive a substantial donation as a result of the day's trading. We were grateful and delighted and another round of drinks was called for, to celebrate. We were astonished by it all and almost completely legless by the time we wobbled our way across Hyde Park, to get the train home.

I regret that I am not able to include a picture of the characters we met on this day! But we had to come back down to earth, after this exciting interlude, and get on with our normal fundraising ventures, which continued, from week to week.

Luckily, we had some committee members who had marvellous ideas about how to go about this and we became very successful at it. Our network of supporters, contributing regular small amounts or even quite large amounts was our bedrock, and we also received occasional bequests. In addition, there were some sponsored runs and other events which raised our profile locally and brought in welcome funds. The local events we held in Devon, became popular and sought after, to the extent that there were cries of protest from our village, when we stopped organising them!

One of the first functions was an Africa Night, in our village hall, at which we served African food. To tell the truth, it was better than most of the food we had managed to source in Zambia, while living on a frugal budget. We found a recipe called Tongabezi chicken, which came from one of the expensive hotels in Livingstone, and we produced our own version, along with a vegetarian option, which was delicious. We usually organised a quiz, a raffle and music from a local choir and other performers, of which there were several. We discovered that the area was full of musically talented people and these nights became so popular that tickets had to be rationed. These fundraising events, although hard work for us, were fun and a good way to bring our local community together.

On one occasion the River Teign rowing club organised a ten mile row at sea, finishing at our local port of Teignmouth, billed as 'Oars for Africa'. It was very successful and certainly raised our profile, locally.

Perhaps the most popular fundraising events were the 'Big Breakfasts' in our village of Bishopsteignton. They were held a few times a year in the community centre and usually raised a good amount of money. People gathered to share food and local gossip, read the papers, and generally socialise, while eating a variety of different breakfasts on offer. The breakfast café lasted all morning, with some people coming in twice, for an early and a late breakfast, or to meet up with different groups of friends. These occasions were an organisational challenge, as we never knew how many people would turn up or what they would eat. One of our Trustees, Helen, became expert at this and she was always able to marshal a small army of willing and hard working volunteers. Because of the popularity of these breakfasts, and other functions, we became very well known as a worthwhile charity, which brought us more donations and offers of help.

We were sometimes invited to give talks to different organisations about Zambia and Alan was particularly good at motivating people to be generous. But the outcome was sometimes unpredictable. On one occasion he mentioned that the nights were cold at certain times of the year and not all the children had blankets. This prompted an explosion of blanket knitting, mainly from local care homes, and soon we were the recipients of a large pile of beautiful multi coloured blankets. The elderly people got very involved and were soon honing their knitting skills to produce teddies, for us to take to Zambia for the children and they were given to the small children at Umwana Kasembe.

Another organisation sent us a van load of enormous soft toys, but they were unsuitable to be taken to Zambia and we had to seek the donor's permission to sell these and donate the profit to our funds. The volunteers who stood in the rain at a Christmas Market selling enormous teddies, did a great job and a good profit was made, but we learned a lesson about how to target our fundraising appeals in future.

In 2006, there was a renewed focus on the prevention of malaria, within Zambia and we organised a campaign to raise money to buy mosquito nets for children. This was quite successful, and a number of bed nets were purchased by the project managers in Zambia. However, it was another example of how the best laid plans can go awry. On our next visit to Zambia, it became obvious that most nets had not been used, or at least, not as bed nets, (although other creative uses had been found for them). Many of the poorest families were living in just one room and had no beds, only a blanket on the floor. There might be several children sleeping together in this way and it was not practical for all of them to sleep under a net. Hellen and the manager at Kantolomba must have been aware of this, but still did their best to encourage any measures to limit the spread of malaria, which caused the deaths of so many young children. Many adults were also regularly afflicted by this debilitating disease. I suffered with it myself one year and was completely floored by it. I was able to access effective treatment quite rapidly, but still found it exhausting and suffered long term effects, which I have described it in another chapter. It gave me just a small insight into the difficulties faced by so many, in Zambia, trying to carry on with their daily lives, to find food for their children, to do their work, while stricken with malaria

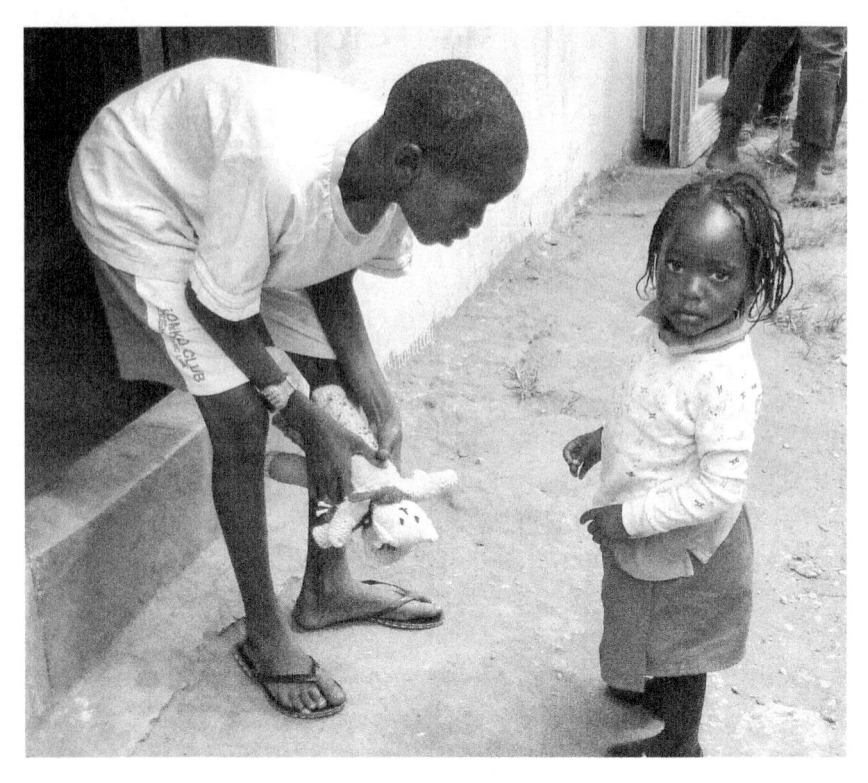

Giving out hand-knitted toys Umwana Kasembe

Chapter 14

Friends in Zambia

As well as our friend Hellen and the Zambian people already mentioned, we met other interesting and hospitable people in our first year in Zambia. Some of them were British, some Irish, or from other countries and most were working with VSO or with other aid agencies on a temporary contract. One of our friends was employed by Irish Aid and was teaching in a college in Lusaka. Another good friend, with whom we stayed in touch, was working with groups of women and was employed by the Canadian government aid programme. Most aid workers, however, were only in the country for a limited time, like us, so it was often to the established long-time residents like Gretta and John that we turned, for help and advice.

John and Gretta Hudson had been in Zambia for many years and had lived and worked there all their long-married life. John was even born in Zambia. We were so fortunate to be introduced to them by the Sisters a few weeks after we arrived, in 1996. We looked after their house and dogs when they were away, from time to time and they became our very good friends. They were an infallible source of information and wise advice on anything to do with the history or politics of the country or who to consult, in any given situation. They had an amazing network of contacts throughout Zambia, which they generously shared with us. Gretta was one of the most energetic, resourceful and hospitable people I have ever met and could turn her hand to most things, from organising a house party, to mending a cooker or handling a gun! We often stayed with them and have many good memories of those times. They were always kind and always helpful.

At the time, John was in the process of writing his book, 'A time to mourn', which was published in 1999. This is an honest, beautifully written and moving account of his experiences as a District Commissioner in the remote north east of Zambia. It is set in 1964, when Zambia, then Northern Rhodesia, was engaged in a struggle for independence. Their house, in Lusaka, was full of papers and books, maps and pictures, as well as his own paintings of landscape and wildlife and we were privileged to be able to have access these. He had many stories to tell from those times and from his long experience working in the Colonial Service and later with the National Farmers Union and in business.

John also had a fund of amusing anecdotes, which he would narrate over dinner sometimes. We found his stories very funny when he recounted them with his dry sense of humour and his quiet, self-deprecating manner. We loved staying with John and Gretta and listening to these stories. We always felt at home there and often met other interesting guests who were staying with them too. They had family in the UK and Ireland and all over the world. I never knew anyone who sent and received so many letters and Christmas cards.

I vividly recall one occasion when they had asked us to stay in their house and take care of their dogs while they were away on a long visit to relatives in England. This was a welcome change for us. The house was large and rambling, with a big garden and a pool and we would have the place to ourselves for a few weeks.

This is what I wrote the following day
It was midnight when we went to bed, after a long hot day. I was feeling jittery; this was our first night alone in the house and it was a big responsibility. Before he left for the airport, John had spent a long time showing us the various padlocks, bolts, shutters, burglar bars and the alarmingly named 'rape' gates. All these had to be locked and bolted every night and the alarm

system set up. The dogs were to be fed and put outside and the security lights turned on. Only the previous year, John told us he had surprised robbers, climbing over the wall at the end of the garden. The contents of the house were their treasured possessions, collected over a long lifetime, and we were responsible for keeping everything safe.

Gretta and John left for the airport, after dark. We were both tired by the time we got to bed and I lay awake for a while, looking at the security light shining through the curtains at the window and listening as the dogs set up their usual sporadic barking, in concert with the neighbourhood dogs.

It must have been some hours later that something woke us.

"Listen, listen, what was that?" Alan whispered, "I think there is somebody in the garden."

"No, no it couldn't be, Alan, the dogs would be barking like mad by now. We must be imagining it. Maybe it's just the wind. Anyway, I'm going to get a drink of water from the kitchen."

As I walked through the house, I passed the frosted glass of the hall window and froze, as I saw the shadow of a man move across it. I stood still, wondering what to do, when, suddenly, I heard Alan's voice in the bedroom. I crept back into the room, to find him talking through the window to a man outside.

"What's going on?"

"It's John, he couldn't get on the flight. Gretta went, but there was no space for him - he had to come back and he doesn't have a key to the house. He got in the gate but has left all the house keys with us."

"Thank goodness it's you, John, we thought you were a robber. Lucky we didn't have your shotgun! You nearly gave me a heart attack."

This was one of many memorable experiences, staying with Gretta and John over the years and we became lifelong friends We also had the invaluable support of the religious Sisters with whom we had worked during our first year. Some of them had been in Zambia for more than 50 years and were highly respected by the communities they lived in. They also had a great support network and were always there for us when we needed them.
Sr Lawrence was an elderly Sister who had been one of the first from her order to arrive in Zambia, 50 years before. She was no longer working as a nurse, but she looked after the community house where she lived and was always pleased to see visitors. Alan was especially fond of her, as she was from the south of Ireland and she always produced tea and cake when we called in! We enjoyed sitting on the veranda with her, looking out on her lovely garden, which was full of birds, and exchanging stories with her. She spoke the local language, so she always had her ear to the ground and knew what was going on; she was an invaluable source of information and a good friend to us.

From my diary
Sr Lawrence told us an incredible story today when we visited, just before Christmas. Apparently she is only just out of gaol! Last Saturday, she was having coffee with two of the other Sisters. They were expecting a parcel from Ireland, from a Sister community there, which should have contained their Christmas cake, baked specially for them. Suddenly there was a loud banging on the gate, followed by shouting, "Police! Open up, open this gate." The gardener opened up and two policemen drove in. They demanded to see Sr Lawrence and said they were arresting her on suspicion of smuggling drugs. A cake had recently arrived, addressed to her and was believed to contain drugs. Of course

she denied ever having smuggled or having anything to do with drugs and explained about the Christmas cake. But to no avail. Ignoring the anguished protests of her fellow Sisters, they took her away in the police car.

She remained calm, as always, remonstrating with the officers and insisting it was all a misunderstanding. Meanwhile, the other Sisters were getting organised. They contacted as many of their community as they could and asked for the word to be passed around. Before long, dozens of Sisters had arrived at the police station, from their own and other religious communities, to protest and demand that Sr Lawrence be released. At this time she was an elderly lady in her eighties, but very strong and determined. Her friends brought a camp bed, blankets and food and drink and one of them insisted on staying in the cell with her. Others blocked the road outside and demanded to be arrested too! The uproar continued late into the night, with the police claiming that the cake had to be tested for drugs. Eventually Sr Lawrence was released, unharmed but very tired. She made light of it, when she recounted the events of that night, saying that it was all a misunderstanding and a bit of an adventure. "I never knew I had so many friends."

"What happened to the cake?" we asked, "well they must have needed the whole thing for testing, my dears, because we never got any of it back."

Chapter 15

The worst and the best

This chapter begins with one of the worst times and ends with a positive story of rebuilding, of progress and of hope for the future. It is hard to recall, looking back, exactly when we began to see that again things were not going well at Kantolomba. When you have invested a lot of time and work and hope and resources in something, you don't want to look for problems. But sometime in 2014 we became increasingly worried that the buildings looked scruffy, that there were always many excuses for things not going to plan. I knew that I could trust Hellen Mpundu to get to the bottom of things and asked her if she would help and advise the managers at Kantolomba. She soon decided to make an unscheduled visit, to see for herself.

As soon as she arrived in Ndola, Hellen went straight to the township and talked to the teachers and volunteers at the school, and to those community members who came to see her. They told her a sad story of the recent dishonesty at the school. The former managers soon made themselves scarce, when Hellen faced them with what they had done. They all resigned.

It gave new hope to the people in that poor community to see Hellen again and they implored her to stay. Not that she needed any encouragement. Hellen was furious to see her beloved project so threatened and was on a mission to rescue it. She faced hostility and threats from the former managers, at first, but she didn't give up and soon she moved back to live there. I asked her where she found the strength to do this and she told me that, for the most part, people were behind her and she knew they would always protect her, while she was moving around or living in the township.

During those weeks, I spoke to Hellen almost every day on the phone and she gave me a detailed and emotional account of all her actions as things unfolded. There were many tears between us. The sense of hurt and betrayal went deep but Hellen found support with her community in Kantolomba, as well as from our daily conversations. I found mine with my group of Trustees and committee. Everyone was upset, especially those who had been in Zambia with us quite recently, but they gave us their unconditional support and practical advice, as always. It did help, but I still felt personally responsible, and I know Alan did too. Thank goodness for Hellen, who rescued Kantolomba back then in 2014 and is still standing.

From this time onward Hellen has worked tirelessly to build up the school, to restore its good reputation and to make up for some of the losses of the previous year.

So, once again, we set to work to rebuild what we had helped to create in Kantolomba. There were things we could have done differently, and maybe we were naïve and too trusting. We always did our best to treat people with honesty and dignity. We hoped that they would be straight with us too and many people were. But the same people who were doing great and inspiring work one day, could be behaving dishonestly the next, which was a hard lesson to learn. For myself I developed a kind of provisional trust, optimistic and hoping for the best, but being aware that things could go wrong and trying to have a back-up plan.

At first, we began to question everything and to doubt much of what had happened and the people we had known. But thank goodness Hellen was still there, going into battle to set things right at Kantolomba, restoring our hope for the future of the children and families there.

She began at first with the women and the smallest children, bringing them into the school for basic care and education. Reading, writing and counting were the priorities for the little ones, to prepare them for going into the main part of the school. She found that the children were eager to learn and were willing to tell her what they wanted. She has always had a wonderful way of communicating with young children. With the women she taught about nutrition, growing vegetables and the essentials of a good diet. She led by example, to encourage them to be more aware of their rights and their potential and to value education for their children, however poor they were.

There were still some people in Kantolomba who did not see the advantage of educating girls, but allowed them to go into early marriages, from the age of 12 or 13. There was also the problem of so called 'sugar daddies'; usually older men who paid money to the parents or guardians, in exchange for a child bride. Sometimes these men would also promise to pay for education and to allow the girl to go to school, but, in practice, this seldom happened. Often girls became pregnant straight away and that could be the end of their education and of their opportunities to progress in their lives.

Hellen decided to allow pregnant girls to attend school and to bring their babies as well, if this could be managed. She continues, to this day, to educate and to fight against the abuse of early marriages on many fronts, because this is still a major problem in Zambia, as in other African countries. A good number of the students, including girls, have now written their grade 12 exams and graduated from the school. Some have even gone on to the Copperbelt University.

There was a problem initially, in bringing the buildings at Kantolomba back up to a decent state and we did what we could to help with that. We managed to raise enough money for a new ablution block, with flushing toilets. This was overseen by Musonda, Hellen's son, who is an excellent builder, and he made a very good job of it, transforming the previously substandard and leaky structures into a smart and functional building. The maintenance of the other buildings is an ongoing issue but Hellen and team do their best to keep on top of it. There are always problems in the rainy season, when the mud brick walls are weakened and sometimes nearly washed away.

Initially, most of the teachers were unqualified, but now all have completed teacher training. Hellen herself has graduated from the Copperbelt university with a degree in education, which we supported financially. The Government of Zambia has, over the last few years, introduced many requirements for teaching, both for buildings and for staff qualifications but has not provided funds for this, so it has put an extra pressure on resources.

Outi Puttonen, mentioned in a previous chapter, is one of the heroines of this story and is still sending funds to Kantolomba, from Finland. This is a lifeline for them, as the school now has more than 600 pupils on the register. Hellen pays the teachers what she can afford from the limited budget and they all choose to work in this school, rather than for a government school, where they might command a bigger salary.

There are now more government schools in the area but our community school was the first to be established in Kantolomba 23 years ago, and is the one which is still chosen by many people. This is because of its high standards of education as well as its caring and inclusive policies and its support for poorer pupils. The school welcomes children with special needs and they are well supported by their peers and by the teachers.

Musonda helps to fund the school, from his business ventures in Lusaka and Chilanga and Hellen, as always, makes the most of any opportunities that come her way to raise funds for school. She herself lives frugally in a small house in Ndola and spends most of her waking hours at Kantolomba or at the farm which they have recently acquired, to grow food and to generate an income.

Once Hellen had established herself in Kantolomba again and had assembled a trusted team of teachers, we met again as a group of Trustees in the UK. We made the decision to put all our capital assets into the rebuilding of the project, now called 'Ulupwa', before handing it over to Hellen and her group of staff, with a plan for phasing out our involvement.

Since then we have, in our different ways, given what we can to support the rebuilding of the project we began so long ago. Despite everything that went before, the story of the last few years has been one of hope, building up again, improving year by year. Our grandson, Nathan, was on a work placement in Zambia in 2014 to 2015, after graduating with a degree in International Development, and he spent some time at Kantolomba school. He reported back to our Trustees that he had seen great progress in the project between his visits and he was able to advise Hellen on report writing, budgeting and accounting, to enable her to apply for and secure funding.

Nathan with Hellen in Kantolomba in 2015

Kantolomba community school is surviving and thriving, and there is a good business plan for the future. Hellen and Musonda have managed to purchase a plot of land, some 4 acres, alongside the main road into Ndola, which they have planted with maize and other vegetables. They have built some kilns and have worked hard to make thousands of building bricks. There is a well on site for fresh water and it is planned to move the hammer mill there, once electricity is connected. They are already supplying all their own needs for food for the school. Hellen is passionate about growing things: it has always been at the centre of her life and I believe she will do well with this, as she has with everything else.

It has given me great pleasure to see the recent photographs and videos, showing the children at the school, who look so well dressed, happy and busy with various activities. The buildings may be in need of maintenance, but what they lack in amenities at Kantolomba community school, they make up for with love and care and a good standard of education.

Hellen sharing lunch with children

Kantolomba 2024

When I returned to Zambia recently and spent some time with my friend, we had chance to look back upon the events of the last few years with more distance and objectivity. We talked about mistakes we made, lessons we have learned and all that has been achieved. We laughed together about the difficult times as well as the good ones. We were two stubborn, determined women then, and I guess we still see each other that way.

As we were talking and reminiscing together, we remembered one particular day which had been very challenging. I can't even remember why now: there were so many stressful days. On this day, we were driving out of Kantolomba in a borrowed van, feeling exhausted and discouraged, when a beat-up old car drove out in front of us. It was garishly painted with the motto 'shit happens'. There was a moment's silence before we looked at each other and then we both began to laugh. We still laugh about that moment, and it has helped us to survive many problems ever since. Along with the school, we are both still standing.

As I come to the end of this story, I remember one of the occasions when Alan and I flew back from Zambia, when I was just getting over a bout of malaria.

From my diary
We flew home, back to London for a break. It felt strange to be cocooned in a small metal capsule, suspended above the earth, unable even to move, strapped into uncomfortable seats, food and drink brought to us as we sat. We were prisoners for a while, with time to think, to watch and to reflect. Going north I could see at first some cultivated fields, rounds of gold carved out of the bush. Over the Congo for hours we floated, looking down on brown rivers and lakes, a dense carpet of forest, looking as it must have done for millennia. In a curve of the river, a cluster of houses at the water's edge, just a small clearing in the forest, with no visible access apart from the river, coiling through the

trees. I thought about the lives of people here. How much have they changed in the centuries? Such a strange contrast between the hi-tech entertainment through the headphones and on the screen while flying over an ancient landscape of endless forest. Eventually forest gave way to desert, even more inhospitable and deserted. No visible buildings or water or roads for hundreds, maybe thousands of miles and a golden glow in the sky.

At last we reached the coast of the Mediterranean, then flew over France. The sun was setting gently in a watery pink and grey sky as we circled London, with a very different river below. The London Eye, the bridges, Canary Wharf, the Isle of Dogs. Meanwhile, on the screen, I watched, or half watched, a film set in Belfast – a boy and a greyhound and the treachery of men. Robert Carlyle playing the anti-hero.

I felt exhausted as we stood in line at passport control and made our way to wait for our baggage to arrive. At last we were through to arrivals and I cried with relief to see my brother waiting there. He was crying too and we hugged for a long time, as we stood there with a river of strangers flowing around us. But eventually we found the car and started the drive back: we talked all the way and it felt good to be home with family again: even chips and tea at a motorway café tasted wonderful.

Yes, it was good to be home, but it would not be long before we returned: Zambia was in our blood. Maybe literally, in my case: the next time I offered myself as a volunteer to give blood, I explained that I had recently had malaria and I was turned down.

Finally, when looking back over the times spent in Zambia, it is the women we knew, who stand out in my memory. Yes, of course, there were some good men, who were honest and hardworking, but it is the women I remember. The brave women of Zambia, some of the strongest, most resourceful and positive people I have ever met. There is a poem I saw pinned up on the wall in one of the houses where we stayed, which I found very moving: I wrote it in my diary when I was staying there, some years ago. It was written, I think, by a visitor to the house, but I have been unable to trace the author. If he or she is around to read this, I hope they will forgive me for quoting it. It has captured something of the struggle and heroism of many women's lives.

Zambian Mother

In the long queue for Mealie meal

With baby on back

Chitenge wrapped when the rains have failed.

On the Bush path,

Barefoot, basket crowned,

To and from the market in barter trade.

On the roadside in the blazing sun

Hawking mats, coloured carpets and earthenware

In her sweat acre, swinging her heavy hoe

Or later, in a good year

with pestle in double grip,

pound, pounding her maize.

Trudging home from the forest

with a pile of firewood on her head

In her mud hut at night wondering

where the next meal will come from

to forestall her children's piteous pleas

and the beckoning grave

Zambian mother

Brave, brave, incredibly brave

and the eighth wonder of the world

the smile on her face.

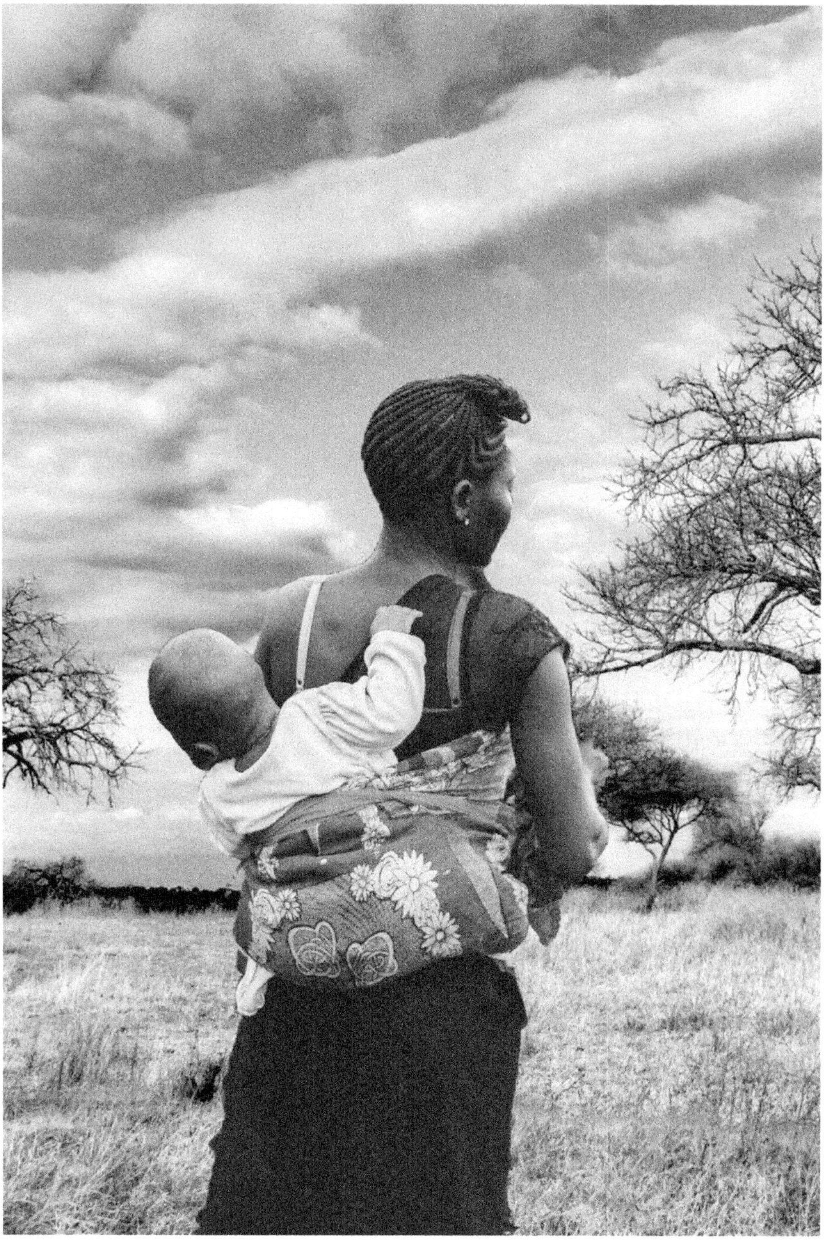

Acknowledgements

There are many people I would like to thank for their help with this book.

Hellen Mpundu, of course, has been a central person and contributor throughout. So too has my husband, Alan, who has shared in everything, listened to many drafts and always believed in it.

My daughter Helen has spent a lot of time helping me to get my multiple writings of the last twenty-five years into a coherent order. I have really valued the honest and insightful suggestions she has made.

Other friends, family and former Trustees, have read and commented on different chapters and have contributed their own words and pictures, in places.

Amanda Dawes took many of the pictures and designed the beautiful cover pages. When I saw them, I began to believe that this book could really begin to exist.

In Zambia there are so many people I would like to thank, who have helped and advised us and who have played a part in this story. My apologies if I do not mention everyone.

We owe a great deal to Sr Elizabeth Dawson and Sr Elizabeth Mooney and to John and Gretta Hudson. They offered us hospitality and unstinting support on many occasions, and we learned so much from them over the years.

Musonda Chipepo, the eldest son of Hellen Mpundu, has been my key contact and helper in organising and getting material together from Zambia for this writing. I could not have finished it without him.

Finally, to Melissa Muldoon, who has worked with me, with great patience and skill, to compile this book and bring it to fruition.

About the Author

Wendy Machin lived for a year in Zambia in the 1990s and made many friends and connections there. She jointly founded a UK charity to support orphans and vulnerable children in Zambia and has spent time working there regularly, over the last 25 years.

In her professional life she was a Social Worker and Project Leader, in Liverpool, Runcorn and Chester and, more recently, in Devon.

Wendy now lives in Devon with her husband, Alan, her partner in all her Zambian ventures. They have five grown up children between them and nine grandchildren. This is her first book.

About the Compiler

Melissa Muldoon is an artist, sculptor, illustrator, graphic designer, editor and compiler.

Previous illustrated books include The Mouse's House, Mouse's Best Day Ever, Mouse And The Storm, T-Rex to Chicken, Moonlight in the Garden, Inside The Broom Cupboard, The Pug in the Helmet, The Hippopotamermaid and Poems to Ponder. Still in the pipeline are numerous mindful books, illustrated works for poetry and many more exciting projects!

Visit www.melissamuldoon.co.uk for more information.

Printed in Great Britain
by Amazon

48984958R00086